THINGS THEY NEVER TAUGHT YOU IN SEMINARY

THINGS THEY NEVER TAUGHT YOU IN SEMINARY

Deborah and James Bushfield

HERALD PRESS
Scottdale, Pennsylvania
Waterloo, Ontario

Library of Congress Cataloging-in-Publication Data
Bushfield, Deborah, 1954-
    Things they never taught you in seminary / Deborah and
James Bushfield.
        p.   cm.
    ISBN 0-8361-3649-7 (alk. paper)
    1. Church management.   2. Clergy—Office.   3. Church work.
I. Bushfield, James, 1952-   . II. Title.
BV652.B875   1994
253—dc20
                                                    93-36050
                                                    CIP

The paper used in this publication is recycled and meets the
minimum requirements of American National Standard for
Information Sciences—Permanence of Paper for Printed Library
Materials, ANSI Z39.48-1984.

All Bible quotations are used by permission, all rights reserved,
and unless otherwise indicated are from the *New Revised Standard
Version Bible,* copyright 1989, by the Division of Christian
Education of the National Council of the Churches of Christ in the
USA; NIV, from *The Holy Bible, New International Version*, copyright
© 1973, 1978, 1984 International Bible Society, Zondervan Bible
Publishers; TLB, from *The Living Bible* © 1971 owned by assignment
by Illinois Regional Bank N.A. (as trustee), Tyndale House
Publishers, Inc., Wheaton, Ill. 60189; KJV, from *The Holy Bible, King
James Version.*

THINGS THEY NEVER TAUGHT YOU IN SEMINARY
Copyright © 1994 by Deborah and James Bushfield
    Published by Herald Press, Scottdale, Pa. 15683
    Published simultaneously in Canada by Herald Press,
    Waterloo, Ont. N2L 6H7. All rights reserved
Library of Congress Catalog Number: 93-36050
International Standard Book Number: 0-8361-3649-7
Printed in the United States of America
Book and cover design by Jim Butti

00 99 98 97 96 95 94 93 10 9 8 7 6 5 4 3 2 1

To our friends

Contents

Authors' Preface

The idea for this book came while we were on vacation. We were driving several hundred miles to rent a house on the ocean, having left our congregation behind us for a week.

We had brought along several books on tape. One (along with the mysteries and dramas) was Mark H. McCormack's *What They Don't Teach You at Harvard Business School.* Listening to this insightful and informative tape on the business world, we began joking how about how pastors need the same kind of advice.

Then it struck us that what we were saying was more than a joke. It was true—pastors *do* need that kind of advice, only in our case seminaries are where they don't teach us all we need to know.

Where do we get the kind of information that is truly valuable in doing ministry? From our friends, our clergy peers. We share experiences, pool knowledge, pass on tidbits of advice as well as occasional horror stories of ministry gone wrong or churches gone sour.

Through such sharing we begin to see potential

pitfalls in our ministry and learn to step around them or prevent their emerging in the first place. We begin to recognize the difference between a small fire that will soon die and one that will blow into a conflagration which, if left unchecked, will consume us.

The information we have gathered here comes from over twenty years of ministry. Some of it we learned through personal experience. Some of it came to us in the form of a gift, of another pastor saying, "Hey, have you tried this? It works!"

However we got it, this material is the practical advice we use and live by. It helps keep us on track. It stops us from taking ourselves too seriously; it keeps us real.

You may not always agree with the views in this book. In fact, they may at times make you angry. But the book will have served its purpose if it challenges you, causes you to examine your own style of ministry, asks you to explore your basic work ethic and the caring relationships your ministry is built on.

Our thanks to all our friends and colleagues who have shared their pain, their discoveries, their faith, and their lives with us as we put together this book.

Special thanks go to Arch and Jerri Hawkins, Ned Steele, Ralph and Lucy Hill, Greg McGarvey, David V. W. Owe, Mark and Brenda Oldstrom, Jack Wolfe, Charles and Beth Myers, and Carolyn Marshall.

Thanks also to all our congregations, who have taught us so much—gently and otherwise.

—*Deborah and James Bushfield*
Bloomington, Indiana

1

Do It During the Honeymoon

You are at a new church. So far the people know what you look like, where you came from, and a little personal history. That's it. They're waiting for you to reveal yourself, to show what kind of leader you are, in what direction you will guide them. They know they are in the midst of change and are willing to accept it—at least as willing as they will ever be.

This situation will last a few months, maybe a few years if you're lucky. By then they will have gotten your number, and resistance will rise as old agendas and power plays reassert themselves.

But for the moment, you're the star. What you say will be listened to. Move carefully and tenderly, but do move. Don't let the end of your honeymoon period come without having tried anything new, without having engaged in something truly exciting and worthwhile, without having led the church into exploring the many possible dimensions of their ministry.

There is an often-repeated piece of questionable advice that goes the rounds when clergy get together and repeat the pseudo-wisdom they've heard on the grapevine. It goes like this: "Don't make any changes during your first year at a new church."

This advice says you should spend the first year getting to know people and the lay of the land. Use the second year to settle in and build a trust level. Then perhaps you can begin to make small, rather insignificant moves in leadership. You can gradually readjust the congregation's direction. You can slowly develop a theological picture of where the church should head—assuming there aren't major roadblocks along the way.

That advice tends to suffocate any opportunity for real change. Sure, it sounds good—go slow, be careful, don't rock the boat. But let's be realistic. If you haven't made significant changes in programming or structure by the second year, it's going to be tough to start then. Remember the law of inertia? It's much harder to start from a stopped position than to keep moving when you're already rolling.

And if you do manage to get into gear after the first year or two, you're going to meet a lot of resistance from the congregation, who thought the status quo was a thing to be maintained, not challenged. They also thought you agreed with them. After all, you hadn't messed with anything so far. Why should you start now?

There's a second problem to consider with this slow-and-easy-does-it philosophy. As one of our clergy friends says, "In the absence of a pastoral leader, a new leader will emerge." You want the pastoral leader to be you. If it's not you, believe me, it will be *someone*, and may well be someone less qualified than you. Trying to assert leadership once someone else has already filled your role will guarantee you many headaches and heartaches.

The third, more obvious, but often overlooked problem with this bide-your-time advice is that you don't have an unlimited number of years in your career. If ordained at twenty-seven, you have about thirty-eight years of active full-time ministry ahead. The average length of a pastorate, depending on location, can range from three to six years. If you move every three years, you will have about twelve pastorates.

You will end up spending at least twelve of your thirty-eight years in ministry waiting for time to pass. You will probably have less than twenty-six years of creative leadership. If you move every six years, you will have about six pastorates. That means a minimum of six years devoted to waiting for those remaining creative years. Either way, approximately 15 to 30 percent of your career will be spent in a holding pattern.

Why not be creative from the beginning? People expect changes when they get a new pastor; that is when they are most accepting of it, even welcoming. It is also the time when they are most pleased with a pastor. It is no accident that the first year has been called the honeymoon.

So how does one begin to work in a church during the honeymoon? It's done in the same way a married couple establishes their relationship during the early part of their marriage. They are tender with each other, considerate of the other's feelings, creative, excited, enthusiastic, dwelling only on the good points, seemingly blind to the other's failures.

We can emulate these qualities during our time of infatuation with a new church. After all, we prefer to see only their good points, and they are looking for the same thing in us. It is our prime opportunity to help them be more than they have been, to build a new life and a new vision of ministry together.

The key word here is *together*. You can't impose your agenda alone. You will need an amalgam of your enthusiasm and leadership heading in a direction the congregation agrees it wants to go.

Ron had moved to his new church in June. He and his family had spent the summer getting to know the people, hosting several parties, accepting every invitation they received, and generally circulating and listening. They were finally beginning to feel comfortable.

Ron knew that in September there would be an increase in attendance (pretty much the case everywhere). He wanted to take advantage of that by sparking the congregation's interest and involvement in a challenge of some kind. But he didn't know what the challenge should be.

In mid-August Ron went on a two-day retreat. During the retreat he prayed, considered options, thought about the conversations he'd had with church members, reviewed their history, and finally returned with a plan. He had a vision of what his sermons and leadership could do to help lead the church toward making a decision. The decision would be a specific direction in ministry, one of the church's own choosing. Based on the congregation's history, Ron had a few directions in mind himself, but he wanted the members to make the final choice.

His first move was to plan sermon topics for the next few months. His goal was to build the church's self-esteem, and to present a series of personal spiritual challenges for individuals. He intended nothing radical, but did want to support a positive mind-set, a can-do emphasis.

Ron's second move was the big risk. He developed a written proposal to take to the board. This proposal detailed the formation of a "futuring" committee. This committee's job would be to meet with him biweekly for a period of three months. They would first read a series of church growth books, and discuss the various theories and programs presented in the books. Their final task would be to develop a mission statement and a plan of action intended to implement the statement in their own church. They would design the plan to be carried out over the next five years.

To Ron's surprise, he had no trouble getting his suggestion past the administrative council, whose members were eager to plan for the future. Ron's idea was novel and simply having a plan was appealing to them. Notice that Ron himself hadn't suggested concrete changes. He had simply invited the church to look at the future and develop its own plan for change.

People became excited. The committee was formed, the books read, the decisions made. Ron was instrumental in helping the congregation see how goals could become reality through specific changes. Once all church participants were informed of the plan and saw the direction they were headed, they vigorously accepted it and moved forward. They were so pleased to realize they had a real direction and a real goal that most of the five-year plan was accomplished in the first year and a half.

Amazing? Ron thought so. But is it really? Aren't we all happier and more productive when we have a goal? If we want to get to a specific location, don't we usually go in a straight line, rather than meandering in all directions?

That was what Ron's church did. They saw their goal, knew it was reachable, and went for it. They had a game plan, and they followed it. Sure, there were slips along the way, and some things were less successful than had been hoped. But overall the church moved forward. The people felt they were starting some significant ministries. They hadn't felt that way in a long time.

Why did they accept Ron's leadership and suggestions so readily? Was it solely the result of an eagerness to be active in ministry? No. It was because they knew they had a strong leader. They had someone who knew what he was doing, someone they could follow.

There are various ways to demonstrate to a church that you know how to lead and are *willing* to lead. Some people can do it simply by personal charisma. Some have an authoritative voice. Others just have the appearance of a leader—tall, well-built, military posture. But what if you have none of these things? Then you have to do it through having guts—the courage of your convictions.

Darlene was a middle-aged minister in her fourth

appointment. She was in her second career, having spent ten years teaching in public schools before recognizing her call to the ordained ministry. Her lower-middle-class church was struggling with accepting a female minister, but her natural friendliness and enthusiasm had gained her respect and quiet support among a large part of the congregation, even though she had been there only four months.

The town was planning a community parade, and churches were allowed to sponsor a float in the parade, although Darlene's church never had. She heard about the parade a week before the monthly board meeting and thought it would be an excellent way to advertise their vacation Bible school and the children's program.

Darlene knew where they could borrow a flatbed trailer. She talked with the Sunday school superintendent about her idea of having some classes ride on the float and throw candy to the crowd. Catching her enthusiasm, the superintendent urged Darlene to get approval from the church council, so they could begin work.

At the council meeting, Darlene explained her plan and outlined its benefits, including making the church more visible in the community and providing an exciting time for the children who would participate.

Just as she was finishing her presentation, one of the longtime members stood up. He didn't look at Darlene, but addressed the chair. "Why didn't this idea go through the education committee?" he demanded. "We have committees to decide these things. *They* should have brought this before us. I don't like the idea of having a female pastor come up with her own schemes and then bringing them to us to rubber-stamp. These things should be done properly, go through channels. I don't like having a program forced on us by the minister."

The entire board shrank down in their chairs. Darlene felt her face go hot, but she also stood and addressed the chair. "May I come forward?" she asked. After being given permission, she went to the podium, "I should have gone through channels," she said, "and I apologize to the education chairperson for not having consulted her, but I knew her committee wasn't scheduled to meet for another two months and the parade is only three weeks away."

She looked at her detractor. "I did in fact go to the Sunday school superintendent, and he agreed with me that it was a good idea. He urged me to come before this body to get approval."

She took a deep breath and let her gaze rove over the entire group. "As far as my coming up with 'schemes,' I'm not going to apologize for leading. As pastor here, it's my responsibility to lead. Now, sometimes I will lead from out in front, and sometimes I will be urging you forward from behind, but I *will* lead this congregation. I *will* fulfill my responsibility." She sat down amidst profound silence.

After the meeting, several people came up to her in the parking lot and said they supported her. During the following week, she got a number of phone calls and visits, also supporting her leadership.

That one showdown, in which Darlene proclaimed her position publicly, won the war for her. No one has given her a serious public challenge since, and the church acknowledges her as leader. She possibly could have been more diplomatic, but the key was that she showed she wouldn't back down from a fight. That was all it took.

There are other, less dramatic things we can do to help the church see us as their new leaders. The first and perhaps easiest is to order new office stationery. See that it has a new theme or more exciting logo—have it changed in some way that makes it look fresher. Make sure that any church signs or boards have your predecessor's name removed and yours put on as soon as possible.

Another and more significant step is to have the chair of the administrative council or board put you on the agenda every month. Some pastors never address the council and thus lose a great opportunity for presenting challenges and educating the congregation in a personal way. You don't have to come up with new programs each month, but do let the council know how things are progressing in your view, or use the time to give encouragement. Be visible.

The third step is to have one-on-one meetings with all committee chairs. Invite them out for coffee, get to know them, ask them how you can help provide resources. Don't volunteer to help run the programs—you don't have time, and it's their job anyway. But do be willing to talk about new ideas and give them information about where they can find appropriate helps for their positions. Become their friend, supporter, and encourager.

The fourth step is to let people know you appreciate them. Write notes to people after they have done a good job. Thank them for their work in the church. You'll find some of these people have never been thanked before.

There are special situations in which a transition in leadership is more difficult than usual. Some churches have unusually long pastorates. This most often happens in very large churches but also occasionally in smaller ones. If you are in such a situation, it can be difficult for the congregation to accept a new minister.

One way to remedy this is to have a public ceremony of installing the new minister. It can be done after the new minister has been in place a few weeks. This is a special service in which a guest speaker talks about ministry, reminds the congregation of its responsibility as God's church, and the new minister is publicly recognized as the spiritual leader of the congregation.

The service should be planned and carried out by the pastor-congregation relations committee. It can feel like self-aggrandizement, but if care is taken to keep God and the ministry of God's church as the central focus, this kind of service can firm up a congregation's commitment to follow new leadership.

Many pastors also find that if they do a particularly good job at more public affairs—such as funerals and weddings—early in their pastorate, the congregation quickly sees them as competent, and others in the community do too.

Whatever you do to take over the reins of leadership in a new church, do it as soon after your arrival as possible. Our friend's warning bears repeating, "In the absence of a pastoral leader, a new leader will emerge." You want that new leader to be you.

One last piece of advice: When you enter a new church and you see there are things you would like to change, when you feel that energy surging through you, and you're ready to go at it with all you've got, there is one thing you must remember:

You're on your honeymoon. Be gentle.

2

The Coffee and Cookie Jump Start

How do you get going in a new place? There are so many people to meet, and, depending on the size of the church, it can take a couple of years to feel you've made good personal contact with everyone. Is there a shortcut?

Yes.

Several weeks before you move in, contact the chairperson of your new pastor-parish committee. Ask that the committee organize a series of one-time informal coffee fellowships in church members' homes. Tell them you will be present at each coffee.

The committee can divide the congregation into groups of about fifteen, and give each host a list of persons to be invited to their home. Have them schedule these coffees to occur during your second month at the new church. It's good to limit them to no more than two a day, with none scheduled on Sundays.

In this way you can visit personally with the entire

congregation in less than a month, assuming you will see about thirty people a day, six days a week, until you have made the entire circuit of coffees. The coffees will provide opportunities for contacts that might have taken a year otherwise.

Have an agenda

During these coffees, ask every one present to tell their names (although you'll also want name tags), an interesting fact about themselves, and how they came to be a member of the church. After each person has shared, you and your spouse can give a brief personal introduction and history. Then ask the church members to list the strengths of the church, and the improvements they'd like to see.

Keep the mood of the meeting optimistic. Don't let it become a forum for criticism or regrets; simply keep reminding people of the question under discussion. It is amazing how quickly you will get an accurate perspective on what the congregation values. So much information comes forth it's difficult to process it all.

Darrel and his wife, Karen, set up these meetings when they first moved to a large suburban church. They had just one coffee scheduled each day, usually in the evenings, with two on Saturdays. For the first three weeks, they had coffee and cookies nearly every evening. After that, the meetings continued in sporadic fashion for the following three weeks. Both Karen and Darrel became very tired of cookies.

However, before the first three weeks were up, they knew they were onto a good thing. And by the end of the entire six weeks, they had met and conversed with more than 80 percent of the membership. They had a clear picture of the church and of many individuals within it. They felt that the six weeks of meetings had advanced them two years in terms of building relationships with a large number in the congregation.

A few months later, during a minor showdown at an administrative board meeting, Darrel was amazed to find a strong majority of support on his side. These people had met with him, eaten with him, shared their dreams. They were now ready to trust his leadership. The atmosphere around church became increasingly relaxed and open to new ideas.

Not all of the credit can go to the coffees, but Darrel felt that they certainly played a major role in the congregation's speedy acceptance of him.

Of course, both Darrel and Karen had to go on a diet after the coffee fellowships were over. And Karen still hasn't regained her liking for cookies, which she feels is a decided advantage.

3

It Is Easier to Obtain Forgiveness than Permission

One of our clergy friends first told us this maxim for getting things done. He had discovered that church people are reluctant to give permission to make changes, but these same people may readily accept a change made without their input. As long as they don't have to be involved in the decision making and it's not going to cost the church much money, they have few qualms about the final decision itself.

Want to paint your parsonage bathroom blue? In most cases, there's no real reason to ask permission. After all, you'll be the one using the bathroom, not a committee. Go ahead and paint it. If they don't like the color, they can repaint it when you move out. It'll probably need repainting then anyway.

But frankly, most church members have no idea what color your bathroom is, and they really don't care, unless you hand the color to them as a decision to be made. Then it becomes their business. And do you really need someone thinking the color of your bathroom is their business?

Carol and her pastor-husband, Ed, had just moved to a new church. At one time, its parsonage had been a showplace, but the green shag carpeting was now matted and smelled of wet dog, and the dining room wallpaper's scenes of life in colonial America (with matching curtains) were somewhat dated.

Carol had dealt with similar problems before—this was her third go-round with green shag carpeting in a parsonage. When the trustee chair, who was giving them the parsonage tour, asked if they saw anything that needed to be changed, she was ready.

"I can see that the house has a lot going for it," she said. "I love the cabinetry and the storage. It's such a practical floorplan."

The chair smiled. "Yes, we're pretty proud of it," he said.

"The only change I'd ask for immediately is the carpeting." She looked pointedly at her husband, who nodded.

"Yes, I'm afraid so," he said. "I guess green used to be considered a neutral, but it sure isn't anymore. And I don't think there's any way to permanently remove pet odors, do you?" he asked the chair.

The chair looked startled and stared down at the carpeting. "You could be right," he said. "Well, I don't know if we have the funds for that. I guess I'd have to check with the finance committee."

The pastor nodded. "Sure. You might want to have it done before our furniture gets here. It's usually considerably cheaper if things don't have to be moved around. A lot easier too."

Please notice that the pastor wasn't really asking permission here. He was making an observation, based on the assumption that they would accede to his wishes. He knew the decision hadn't been made yet, but this early request was likely to be honored. Churches are always most ready to make changes when a new pastor comes and they want the new parsonage family to be happy.

The trustees toured the parsonage later that week. Most of them hadn't been in it in years, and they were surprised that it didn't quite match up to their memories of a showplace. After the tour, they decided it did need new carpeting, not only in the livingroom, but throughout. When they conveyed this news to Carol, she sent them a sample of what she considered neutral carpeting. They liked her choice and purchased it for the entire parsonage.

A few weeks after they moved in, Carol knew she really couldn't live with the dining room wallpaper. Looking at red-and-brown scenes of native Americans greeting pilgrims with gifts of food was okay for Thanksgiving, but a little too much for every other day of the year. Fortunately, there were several stains on the wallpaper and the matching drapes were very faded, so Carol didn't feel even a twinge of guilt when she rented a wallpaper steamer and removed the dining room wallpaper.

Now this was a risk, and one that not all of us would be willing to take. She didn't know who had first put up the old wallpaper, or how her actions would be received. But the wallpaper was so ugly she was willing to bear any repercussions caused by its removal.

After the paper was down, Carol informed the trustees she would be repapering and offered to hang the new paper herself if they would pay for it. They willingly agreed, and though it took her many hours of work, she finally had the house decorated to reflect her family's personality. She had made it their home.

Carol has made similar changes in several other parsonages and has never had a problem. Why does this work for her? Because she follows the old scout rule: Always leave a place in better condition than you found it. She has good taste, does an excellent job papering and painting, and is careful to repair any damage or stains.

Set your own vacation

The forgiveness-rather-than-permission rule works for things other than parsonage improvements. Setting vacation times is one of them. It makes sense for you to set your vacation time yourself, rather than to ask a committee when they think it would be convenient for you to be gone. Set your vacation for when you expect to need it the most, or when it would work best for your family with the exception, of course, of major church holidays. Churches take a dim view of ministers who take off during Advent or Easter week.

You'll find there are many other applications for this rule. It presents the least number of problems when the changes are fairly insignificant and don't affect the congregation at large.

Know what the limits of forgiveness are

Sometimes, however, you may want to use this

rule on something that isn't so minor. Roger was the new pastor at a six hundred member church that had a one-line telephone system with call waiting, heavy black dial telephones, and a secretary's office thirty feet down the hall.

The old intercom system between his office and the secretary's no longer worked; it merely delivered static. The secretary had devised a system of turning the system on twice, thus sending two bursts of static into his office to tell him when he was wanted on the telephone. The one-line system was often overloaded, and many of his calls were interrupted by the call waiting system.

After a few months of dealing with the inadequate phone system and losing several members' conversations to call waiting, Roger was fed up. It so happened that his secretary was going on a four-day vacation, and Roger would also be out of town for part of the week and weekend. However, there were some crucial illnesses in the church, and Roger wanted to be able to get messages in case he had to make a hasty return.

Roger made use of the rule. He knew there was extra money in the budget for office improvements, and he felt that the illness situation was serious enough to warrant immediate action. He had an answering machine installed on the church line, one he could access from any touch-tone phone.

The church board had been debating the possibility of getting an answering machine for years, but they couldn't get over their reluctance to talk to a tape recorder, so nothing had ever been done. Roger's action took the matter out of their hands.

Although a few people were unhappy at listening to a recorded message when they called during the evenings or the secretary's time off, all agreed it was better than not getting through at all. Roger's conscientiousness about returning all calls made to the answering machine helped make the transition easier.

Once the first improvement had been made, it wasn't difficult to see that the entire phone system needed to be modernized. Roger had a church trustee make preliminary investigation into having a two-line phone system installed, along with new touch-tone handsets. The trustee did her homework and had two bids ready for the next board meeting. Roger pointed out the obvious necessity for change, and the improvements passed with little discussion and no dissension.

If Roger had first asked permission about the answering machine, likely nothing would have been decided for several months. His first independent decision made all subsequent group decisions easier.

However, this advice comes with a warning. Don't succumb to the temptation of adopting this rule as a way of thinking. The seventy-times-seven mode of forgiveness has not yet become common in our churches. The rule works best when the decisions have no financial impact on the church or result in relatively small expenditures. If Roger had gone ahead and ordered an entirely new phone system on his own authority, he might have found himself in the middle of an ugly confrontation with the council. However, he knew how far to push the rule. He knew where the line of challenge was and he didn't cross it.

How to decide

When is a good time to use the rule? When—

- the change affects you more than anyone else,
- the change is not a big expenditure,
- the change is obviously for the better,
- the change was inevitable anyway, given enough time.

Sometimes it makes sense to relieve people of decisions they'd rather not have to make. If you know you can make the decision and you can bear the resulting fallout, it may be good to remember it often *is* easier to obtain forgiveness than permission.

4

Foxes Have Dens . . . Birds Have Nests

Many pastors live in parsonages, although some now have housing allowances and may rent or own their own homes. While each of our houses is different, they all have one thing in common—they are where we live. They are where we go to relax, to retreat, to entertain, and to be truly ourselves. They are not just annexes to our churches. They are our homes.

Separation of church and home

One young pastor realized the value of a strict separation between church and home during his first year of ministry. Jack was in seminary and serving a rural two-point charge. Although he'd worked as a youth minister during college, this was his first real appointment.

Jack liked living in the church's parsonage, but after he had lived there a few months, he came up with a list of several small repairs that needed to be made. He also wanted to discuss the lawn care equipment with the trustees and to recommend an upgrade. The parsonage lawn covered about two acres and the only equipment was an old nineteen-inch power mower. It usually took him between four and six hours to cut the grass, and he often had to spend most of his day off doing yard work.

Jack decided to invite the trustees over to his home for a meeting. He felt that it would be hospitable, that they could all gather around the dining table as friends, and that since the parsonage itself was the topic of discussion, it was even appropriate.

At the meeting everyone was comfortable. Homemade cookies were on the table, coffee cups were full, and the meeting went on and on, as meetings tended to do in that church. Nine o'clock came. Ten o'clock. People relaxed and voices rose, mostly in acclamation of how the four-room parsonage was a palace compared to the previous one, and how lucky Jack was to live in such a nice house.

The tone gradually became parental. Suggestions were made about how Jack should keep the gutters cleared, the importance of spring cleaning, and the benefits of mowing the two-acre lawn at least twice a week during the growing season. Though Jack kept trying to steer the conversation toward dealing with parsonage repairs and a larger, more efficient lawn mower, the trustees were not in a decision-making mood. They seemed to feel they were out for a social evening. They told old parsonage stories and discussed their own home renovation problems.

When everything had been said and nothing done,

the meeting finally broke up around eleven o'clock. The trustees heaved themselves to their collective feet, and thanked Jack for the cookies and the good time. Then they left.

Jack sat alone amid the cookie crumbs, frustrated and hurting. The real pain came from the fact that he'd felt ineffective and vulnerable in his own home, on his own territory. He'd dealt with slow-to-move committees in the church without any problem, but it felt much more serious and personal when it occurred in his own dining room. It took Jack a long time to recover his enthusiasm for meetings and his belief that he could motivate people. He hasn't had a business meeting in the parsonage since.

We don't want to imply that one shouldn't have church groups and gatherings in the parsonage. Pastors need to practice hospitality. But the key difference is in hosting social events rather than business meetings.

Have parties, not meetings

At our various parsonages, we've had women's groups, choir groups, Sunday school groups, and even the pastor-congregation relations committee over. But the groups always came at our invitation only and had a social purpose. When we do have an administrative group over, such as the pastor-congregation relations committee, we invite their whole families and make it a picnic. We grill hamburgers, drink lemonade, and play toss-the-water-balloon. We don't conduct business.

It is good and even necessary to be hospitable, but don't waste your hospitality on the gritty work of administration. It won't be appreciated, and it will turn your home into a church extension. There are cases where church members become so accustomed to using the parsonage that they regularly schedule meetings in the living room; they assume that since it is their property, it is theirs to use.

Please don't let this happen. If it has happened during the previous pastor's term, don't unpack until you've made it quite clear that it will no longer be convenient for them to hold their meetings in your home. You have other plans for it. Be kind, cheerful, even humorous. But most of all, be firm. It could save your marriage. It will certainly save your sense of privacy and peace of mind.

Janet and Bill were being shown the parsonage they would be moving into with their three young sons. It was a big house on a hill next to the church. It had a large drive-out basement garage and French doors that opened out of the basement level onto a nice-sized patio.

The chairman of the trustees took them through the house, but skipped the basement.

"Wait," Bill said as they seemed about to leave. "I'd like to take a look at the downstairs."

"Well, that's just the thrift shop," the trustee said. "Pretty crowded down there, what with the racks of clothes and everything."

"A thrift shop?" Janet asked. She glanced at Bill, who looked as startled as she was.

"Yes, Pastor Henderson and his wife weren't using the basement, so we set it up down there three years ago. Makes it pretty handy to the church," the trustee said.

Bill sighed, then summoned a grin. "It sounds real handy. The only problem is, it's *too* handy to where we'll be living with three small boys. Those kids need room to play and bounce around when it's too cold or too wet to be outside. The living room upstairs isn't really suitable. We need the basement for living space."

The trustee looked disturbed. "But where will be put the thrift shop?"

Janet smiled. "Where was it before?"

"In the church basement." He looked doubtful. "I guess we could move it back, if we had to."

Bill nodded and grinned at the trustee. "That's good. The only other solution that seems possible is if someone else nearby might want to have it in *their* house. Know of anyone?"

The trustee shook his head. "No way. Nobody'd want all that stuff in their house, have to tend it, lock and unlock for people." He stopped and suddenly looked embarrassed.

Bill spread his hands. "Well, that's where we are, too. Glad you understand."

The trustee nodded and finally returned Bill's grin. "Yeah, I see your point. I don't have any kids, and I sure wouldn't want that mess in my house. We'll have the basement cleaned out before you move in."

It's best to try to handle these situations with humor, as Bill did. However, firmness may often be necessary in order to preserve your privacy when you first move into a parsonage.

Speaking of privacy, you may want to find out early who has a key to your parsonage and under what circumstances they feel free to use it.

Cindy and her husband, Rob, had moved to a new church. Rob was the pastor and their parsonage was right next door to the church. One Sunday morning a few weeks after they moved in, Rob had already gone to the church to prepare for his sermon, and Cindy was in the parsonage getting dressed. She heard the back door lock click and the door open. Thinking it was her husband come back for some reason, she went out into the kitchen in her slip.

There stood two male church trustees.

Cindy stared at them, stunned. They murmured clumsy apologies about wanting to check on the water heater (which *had* been acting up), and hurriedly let themselves out, stumbling over each other in their clumsy haste to get out the door.

Cindy was both embarrassed and furious. When she told Rob of the episode after church, he was even more furious. That evening he called the trustee chair. He demanded and received all extra keys to the parsonage. Then he changed the locks.

Parsonage repairs and renovations— quality of life

Committees are notorious for wanting to save money, to get the lowest bidder, to just make do with what already exists. This is fine for committees. They don't have to live with the results of their decisions. Pastors and their families do.

Ellen was the first female appointed to serve as pastor in the small-town church's eighty-year history. She and her husband were shown a parsonage that was large, newly carpeted, and quite adequate for their needs.

However, during the initial tour, Ellen noticed that the kitchen countertop had an eight-inch hole in it. It looked as if someone had set fire to the center of the countertop, then cut away the burned plastic down to the underlying wood. She was reluctant to point it out. After all, the church had just spent a fortune on new carpeting.

Then she pictured her family using the kitchen, eating there, having holiday gatherings, inviting friends over for dinner. She knew that the countertop as it was would always be a nagging annoyance.

While they were still in the kitchen, Ellen suggested that the trustees get a new countertop before she and her family moved in. The committee consisted of three people, one woman and two men. The men looked dubious, but the woman immediately went over to the damaged area, and exclaimed that it was a disgrace and would certainly be replaced right away. It was.

If Ellen had not mentioned the countertop, the woman on the committee might not have noticed it. Likely Ellen's family would have lived with the marred countertop for the entire length of their appointment there. It would have been an ever-present reminder that this was not really their house and they had little control over their quality of life.

When to start

The time to see to it that your family has a decent quality of life is before you move in. When you are first shown the parsonage, look around carefully. Ask questions. If you have three children and the clothes dryer doesn't work, the quality of your family life will suffer. Make clear to the trustees and pastor-parish committee (and any denominational supervisors or overseers) that any broken parsonage appliances will need to be repaired or replaced before you move in. Now is not the time to be shy.

Pastors usually find that churches are most willing to make changes in the parsonage at the very beginning of their term. To wait often results in no repair. Besides, at the beginning of a pastorate, the church will be so caught up in getting used to a new parsonage family that they will be more likely to take renovations in stride. They find it logical to quote the saying "A new broom sweeps clean," and they will accept improvements as a matter of course.

If you see a need or problems, remember that you are the one who will usually have to make the suggestions for a remedy.

Making the parsonage your home

What does living in a parsonage come down to? It comes down to treating it as if it were your own house, a house that you have a large investment in and which you want to keep in good condition. It also comes down to making it your own territory, physically, emotionally, and socially. And it especially comes down to making the parsonage a place of love, nurture, and hospitality. After all, that's the only way you can make the parsonage truly your home.

5

It's a Tough Job, but Somebody's Got to Do It: Being the Boss

Why don't they teach management courses in seminary? Places of higher theological education seem to assume their students will not be managing large numbers of volunteers and small numbers of creative, temperamental paid staff. Or perhaps they think we already know how to be managers.

They are wrong on both counts. Ministers serving churches in pastoral capacities are also managers. And although the numbers are rising, few of us are entering second careers, stepping into ministry after abandoning a career as managers in a more secular business. So how do we learn the necessary skills? Unfortunately, it is usually by trial and error—and sometimes heavy on the error.

Our theological education may often hamper rather than help us in this regard. Throughout our training, we bathe in an atmosphere that promotes humility—we understand that we are to be the servant of the congregation, that she who would be first shall be last. This leads us to think of ourselves in very humble terms. And many of us find that a humble manager is an ineffective manager.

Small churches versus big churches

Small churches and big churches are two different species. Don't let anyone tell you they aren't.

Small churches each have their own way of doing things, their own administration. Usually the same people have had control for a long time. They feel strongly that it is their church, and you are just an interim pastor who will be gone someday.

You can't really buck their system and be successful, especially not at first. You need to work into it, to see how it runs, and to begin making your suggestions privately to the movers and shakers. In a small church, a public confrontation is a lose-lose situation. Everyone is related, the church really is a family, and you can't afford to upset the entire family.

You still have to lead, but you have to do it underground. Small churches are self-protective. Being small makes you aware of how fragile your existence may be. You don't want some outsider coming in and messing with a program that is maintaining itself. And that's the challenge. The small church is usually in a maintenance mode. Growth is not on the agenda, unless there is new growth in the local community.

How can you lead people who aren't sure they want either a leader or growth? It's hard, maybe impossible in some places. But be persistent. Keep your sense of humor. Be gentle. Above all, love the people, no matter how stubborn they may seem to be.

There are a few ways you can soften up a small church so you will be heard.

> **1. Praise them a lot.** Point out all the good things in their program, the good people in their congregation, the history of the church.
>
> **2. Tell them they're friendly.** You are trying to build a new self-image for them, and being a friendly place is what every church wants to be. Besides, if they begin thinking of themselves as friendly, they'll soon become more open. Maybe.
>
> **3. Deal directly with the leadership.** Consult them. Ask their advice. Make them your allies. Without their support, you can do nothing.
>
> **4. Keep a clear vision of ministry ever before them.** Let them know that even though they may be limited in what they can do, God still has a dream for them.

The one constant about small churches is that they are more resistant to change than most big churches. You may stay at a small church a few years and decide you can't ever really lead this church in the direction you think it needs to go. If this happens, and you realize you can't live with this knowledge, it's time to leave. But be of good cheer, you will have learned a lot. And be assured that your whole career won't be like your first church. If it were, not many of us would remain in the ministry.

The big church—
a combination of smaller churches

This sounds strange, but it's true. Whenever a

church gets too large for each member to know everyone else, small groups develop within the congregation. These groups usually center around certain Sunday school classes, the women's group, or various social groups. But they are there, each with their own agenda for the church.

Some of these groups will gain predominance in the church after several years, and the entire congregation may seem to adapt itself to the personality and goals of a comparatively small number. At other times, there may be friction between the groups as a younger, newer group begins its rise to dominance and starts to instigate change.

It takes a strong leader to unite these small groups into one large, effective body of ministry. This involves management of staff and volunteers, as well as coordination between the spiritual and administrative arms of the church. The pastor needs to be that leader.

In the absence of a leader, a leader will emerge

Allison learned the importance of being a leader when she moved to Grace Church—a 350-member congregation in a suburban area. It was a lively, growth-oriented congregation, made up largely of white-collar professionals and those who owned their own businesses. They were in a growing community and were considering building a new sanctuary, as well as offering more programs to attract new people. So much was going on that Allison's first instinct was to sit back and observe.

What she observed was a power struggle.

Everyone had a cause, a good idea the church ought to pursue. Several eager members were doing programs on their own, without approval from the church council. Three different times during the first week, individuals came to see Allison and tell her their ideas of where they thought the church was headed.

Allison was overwhelmed. She didn't want to take sides and wasn't sure she should. After all, she was the pastor, she was supposed to help them spiritually, not become a parent who made decisions for them. So she refused to interfere or give direction. Church meetings became an agony as many would-be leaders struggled to promote their own agendas. Conflicts arose and feelings were hurt.

Following her basic belief in letting all members be self-determining, Allison limited her leadership to the spiritual side of congregational life. She let the administrative side be handled by the lay people. She felt if they got right spiritually, the administration would take care of itself. She kept preaching and visiting, trying to placate parishioners everywhere she went.

Her stomach became very sensitive, and she always woke up with a headache on Sunday mornings. Each week she knew she'd have to ward off complainers who would corner her in the office as she was trying to prepare for the service.

After a few months, attendance began to drop. People told Allison that they just couldn't stand the bickering, the meetings had become battlegrounds, and they needed to go to a church where there was more of a spirit of love.

The council turned to Allison for direction, but she

refused to take part in the controversy. After all, it was their church, not hers. It wouldn't be right for her to make their decisions for them.

In a panic, the council elected Larry as their new chair. Larry had started his own business thirty years before and had a reputation for getting things done. He was a good businessman.

At the first meeting Larry chaired, he took control. He let the church know it would run like a business; he would be the CEO. He demanded full financial accounting, down to the penny, from every committee, and he decided which expenditures were frivolous. He got the board to cancel many fledgling programs and to streamline the chain of command, so that he had final okay or veto power over all finances and programming. He even had himself put on the pastor-congregation relations committee as an at-large member.

Finally Larry told Allison he wanted an accounting of her hours each week, and he wanted to know every time she left town for any reason, even if just to go out to dinner in a neighboring town. After all, she was supposed to be on-call twenty-four hours every day. In addition, he wanted an outline of her sermons in advance, so he could make suggestions and deletions.

This last demand finally woke Allison up. Her position as leader, as shepherd of the flock, had been usurped. She was now viewed simply as an employee. And it was her own fault. She finally realized the great truth about leadership we mentioned in the first chapter:

In the Absence of a Leader, a New Leader Will Emerge

It would be an uphill battle for Allison to regain any of the ground she had lost, and she would have to fight for every inch. It was a battle she never did quite win at that church.

At the time Allison left four years later, Larry was still calling the shots. Though his power had been modified, the congregation took Larry's leadership for granted, and for the most part suffered silently. After all, he was a man who got things done. He had settled many major controversies that had threatened to tear the church apart. They couldn't complain too much. He knew how to manage people.

How could this problem have been prevented? What information did Allison lack that cost her four years of anxiety and unfruitful ministry?

Taking the helm

Allison didn't take the leadership role offered to her when she assumed the pastorate. In her willingness to step back and observe, she became so objective she disengaged. In her dislike for determining actions others should take, she gave no direction. Her church became a ship without a captain. No wonder various mutinies ensued and a pirate took control. It was either that or watch the ship go down.

Being a pastor requires leadership, but not just spiritual leadership. It also requires a kind of practical leadership of resources, staff, and volunteers that isn't taught in seminaries. Allison was doing only half the job.

Getting a vision

There's a quote from a wise old bishop that goes something like this: "A church's vision will never exceed that of its pastor."

Daniel is minister of a medium-sized growing church. Every three months, Daniel goes out of town on a three-day retreat. During this time, he prays and plans the sermon topics for the next three months. He includes Scripture texts, key sermon points, and possible hymns. He tries to get a feel for where God is leading his church and what they need to hear to help them get there. If any program ideas come to him, he jots them down, then follows up on them when he returns home.

Daniel has found that this quiet time, away from interruptions, offers real renewal. It also greatly helps the weekly work of preparing a worship service. The chief bonus is that during these retreats, his mind is open to new ideas, and he often comes home with a new, clear direction—a vision of where his church ought to be heading.

When he gets home, he shares the vision. He tries it out on people from different groups within the congregation and uses their input to refine and strengthen it. As the church's involvement grows, it becomes *their* vision. And a church with a vision becomes a powerful entity.

Loyalty—to the senior pastor and to the vision

When you first go into a church, people assume you will be their new leader. You've more or less got the support of the church at large. How do you deal with those who have their own group of supporters, the other church staff, hired by your predecessor or *their* predecessor, whose ideas about their positions may be different from yours? How do you mesh all the different agendas to make a coherent whole?

We talked earlier about vision. This is the key.

Your staff must not only share your vision for the church, but they must be loyal, both to it and to you. And they need to know that this is what is expected to them.

Working with creative people— Where there's light, there's heat

It takes a strong ego to work with strong people, and to give them the freedom they need to do their jobs well. Successful pastors know they can't do the job of managing a church alone; they have to have good people to grow a good church. It's often a temptation to do the work yourself, but as the staff needs to be loyal to you as their head, you need to be loyal to them, and let their own leadership develop.

Creative people are often temperamental. They tend to be fast thinkers, frustrated at having to wait for plodders to catch up. The handicap that comes with this kind of frustration is that, because they tend to want things to move quickly, they may lose interest in a project while it's being discussed and having the kinks worked out—they're often not good at follow-through. In order to stay interested and see their ideas come to fruition, most creative people need a manager. In the church, that becomes your job.

If you want to help your staff be as creative and effective as possible, here are a few guidelines.

> **1. Give them support.** We're not just talking about your support here. Pair them with practical helpers, people good at following up an idea, who can see how it should be implemented. Give their project legs.
>
> **2. Give them guidelines and deadlines.** They may need your help to see all the steps it will take to get a program off the ground. They may also need you to tell them when it needs to be completed. Creative people, like most of us, work best under pressure.
>
> **3. Hold them accountable.** People need to know that they have real responsibility, that their jobs are important. Don't rescue them or accept excuses as to why they didn't perform promised work. Challenge them. Let them know you hold them in high regard, and expect their best.
>
> **4. Be clear about your own position.** As pastor, you're a key leader. In many congregations you are the supervisor of the other workers. This has to be made clear.

Along with the above advice, we add that once people are going on a project, you should let them go. If they are sharing the same vision with you and the church, a vision hammered out together, they should be allowed to complete it without having someone else tinkering with it along the way. Let them reap the rewards of having done it themselves.

The tough part of the job

Mark was moving into a church whose secretary had been on staff for eighteen years. Rita was like the dragon at the gates. She had run the church office and other staff during her entire tenure. The pastor who was retiring told Mark he would need to get rid of Rita. Mark suggested that the retiring pastor fire her before he left, but his suggestion was refused.

Mark knew he had three choices. He could try to keep Rita happy, expend a lot of energy earning her trust, and put up with her office rudeness and tart remarks; he could overload her with work and try to get her to quit; or he could be blunt, tell her what behavior he expected, and let her know she could leave if she didn't like it.

Mark decided to wait until he met her and had worked with her to make any decision.

Things started out calmly enough, with Rita letting him know she was very competent, and he wouldn't have to worry about things getting done on time. However, her rudeness to visitors and to the other staff was noticeable. Despite Mark's quiet talks with Rita in his office concerning her behavior, she didn't see that there was any problem.

Soon Mark realized that the working situation was becoming intolerable. Rita often said things that drove the undersecretary to tears and made church members avoid the office if at all possible.

After a couple of months, Mark had a meeting with the trustees. He asked for a computer system and explained in detail how it would help with everything from the weekly bulletin to keeping track of the budget. They were sold.

When Mark told Rita and the other secretary that they would soon be getting a computer with two terminals and a state-of-the-art printer, Rita blew up.

"Why wasn't I consulted?" she demanded, as the

undersecretary averted her eyes. "We don't need that. It's a waste of good money! I won't use it, I'll tell you that right now." She folded her arms, staring challengingly at Mark.

He nodded. "I thought you might feel that way. If you feel it's too much for you to learn, we can shift responsibilities around here. The other secretary can use it and we can allot you the jobs that are left, such as answering the phone, and keeping track of the calendar. No, wait, I think I'd like the calendar put on the computer. Well, no matter, we'll find something for you to do."

He walked into his office, leaving her sputtering. After ten minutes there was a knock on his door. Before he could answer, the door opened and Rita sailed in.

"I know what you're trying to do," she said. "You think just because you're the new pastor, Mr. High and Mighty, that you can call all the shots around here. Well, that is *my* office out there," she said, pointing a finger back toward the door, "and I say what goes. And we're not getting a new computer, and you can tell that to those spineless trustees!"

"Please have a seat, Rita," Mark said. He waited, watching while she seemed to struggle with herself over whether or not she was going to sit down. Finally she didn't sit, shaking her head in an angry denial.

"All right, then you can hear this standing up. That office," he pointed, as she had, "is not yours. And it's not mine. It belongs to the church. The people who pay your salary are entitled to the best possible return for their money. If they decide that means installing a computer for more efficiency, then that is what will happen."

Rita started to interrupt, but he raised a hand.

"I'm not finished yet. The people who pay your salary are also entitled to a friendly greeting when they come into contact with any of the staff from this church. That includes phone contact or personal contact. No more rudeness will be tolerated in this office, either to church members or to other staff. This is a Christian organization; it will present a Christian witness. If you can't abide by these standards and won't do the work assigned on the equipment assigned, then you may want to seek employment elsewhere."

Rita's face was dark red. "Are you firing me?" she asked.

"No, I'm just telling you how things are going to be around here from now on. Would you like it in writing?"

Rita spluttered and finally came out with, "You can't get away with this. I'll have you out of here so fast you won't have time to pack. Mark my words." She gave him a last malevolent look and hurried out the door.

Mark followed her to the outer office where she had just picked up a telephone. She stared at him as he came over to her desk.

"Listen a minute," Mark said, directing his glance to the other secretary. "Rita and I have just had a discussion on appropriate church office behavior. I explained that, above all, we are to present a Christian witness here. We are to be kind, patient, and caring. Also, we are to do assigned work on assigned equipment.

"I believe these are reasonable requirements for those desiring continued employment in a church office. If anyone here is unable to fulfill those requirements, I would suggest they seek another position— before they are asked to." He glanced at the two secretaries and summoned a smile. "That's all. Let's get back to work, shall we? Oh, and Rita, no personal calls unless it's your lunch hour, okay?" He returned to his office.

Rita, tight-lipped, gathered her purse and jacket and silently left the office. She never returned. A week later a few church members sponsored a retirement party for her. Attendance was low.

Mark took a risk here. He didn't really know the strength of Rita's following. If she had had a large group of church friends, she could have caused a deep rift in the congregation. If she had been a church member, the risk would have been even larger.

However, Mark knew that the current situation was too disruptive to his work and to the overall atmosphere of the church to let it remain. After a few months, the handful of members who were disgruntled by Rita's leaving accepted the situation. The office became a place where people knew they would be welcomed and comforted.

What do you do when a situation such as this one presents itself?

What Mark didn't do, and what he probably should have done, was to consult the congregation-staff relations committee. It is often theoretically a committee's responsibility to deal with staff members. However, it is usually up to the pastor to act as manager.

Always try to settle problems by talking them through. If two staff members are at odds and it is affecting their work and the work of the church, have them try to work it out together. If that doesn't work, sit down with them and try to come to some resolution of the problem. If *that* doesn't work, bring in the staff-congregation committee. If they still seem unwilling to resolve their differences and are not inclined to work together in peace, establish a treaty that if broken will result in dismissal for the party who breaks it.

Nobody likes being the tough guy, but that's often what the pastor's job demands if the church is going to run smoothly. It's not a pleasant responsibility, but it's an important one. And after all, that's why you get the big bucks (sometimes!).

One last note: Get a support group

It's sometimes lonely at the top, but it needn't be. You may find it helpful to get into a sharing group composed of people outside of your church. Let yourself become friends with folks who don't mind if you fail, and who will be honest enough to tell you when you do.

Other pastors are good for this—they've failed a few times themselves and know where you're coming from. In any case, it is good to find a group where you can be yourself, warts and all. Unfortunately, you usually won't find this group in your own church, but do try to find it. It can prevent the head from getting too big and keep it in touch with the feet.

6

The Midnight Phone Call

It was 2:00 a.m. when the phone rang. Diane didn't really come awake until the third ring. She couldn't find the phone for another few seconds. "Hello," she said, trying to sound alert, but hearing the slur in her voice.

"Pastor Hankins?" an unfamiliar male voice said. "I'm Carl William's AA buddy. Carl fell off the wagon tonight. He's threatening suicide and wants to talk to you."

Diane woke up instantly. "Where are you?"

"At Carl's house. He called me from a bar and I brought him over here. Can you come right over? He seems pretty desperate."

Diane heard a low moaning in the background. Could that be Carl?

The man spoke again. "Listen, Pastor Hankins, I better get back to Carl. He's in the other room and I'm afraid to leave him alone. How long will it take you to get here?"

"No, wait," Diane said quickly. "Get him to the

emergency room at the hospital. Tell him I'll meet him there."

"But he wants you *here*. I don't know if he'll want to get out in the car again. He's been kind of sick—"

She thought quickly. Two men in a house at 2:00 a.m. One of them drunk, threatening to hurt himself—the other a stranger to her. "No, I can't come to his house. I'll meet him at the emergency room. Tell him I'll be there in twenty minutes."

She hung up, hoping Carl's friend was strong enough to get him to the hospital, even against his will. If they didn't show up soon after she got there, she'd have to call the sheriff.

Diane was able to think quickly in a tough situation. She reacted so well because she'd been through similar scenes a few times before.

What if you don't have this kind of experience and you get a late-night phone call? You wake up confused, disoriented, and plunged into someone's real or perceived crisis. How do you assess the situation and decide what to do?

It is helpful if you've thought about your possible reactions ahead of time. There are always three choices: get up and leave immediately, stay on the phone and try to work it out with a follow-up visit the next day, and the real tough one—go with your instincts at the time, depending on the desperation of the caller and the crisis.

Get up and go

Get-up-and-go situations are easy to assess. They include cases of death, suicide attempts, rapes, serious accidents, and sudden illnesses such as heart attacks. These fall basically under the category of emergency calls to a hospital.

Many pastors also feel it is important to go when a child makes the request, no matter what the reason. Even though the parents may say things are okay and you don't need to come right away, if the child wants you there, you may choose to go. From the age of about four on up through college, children are making relationships and identifying those they feel they can trust. If they have identified you as a trusted figure, you don't want to let them down. It may strongly affect their later spiritual development.

Deal with it on the telephone

There are times you probably don't need to rush out. Things will keep until morning.

These include situations when someone calls who is intoxicated (but not threatening physical harm to anyone), when a spouse calls and says a mate is drunk (again, no physical threats, just the hope that you will do something), and when people are worried about their job, money, or love life and want to deal with it now, at midnight, when they're most upset.

There is one other, more nebulous, situation. That is when someone calls and will say only, "I have to see you—it's urgent." The person will not reveal the reason but just repeats the need to see you.

In this case, don't go until told why. Say, "I have to know." Keep saying this until the reason is finally revealed. Of course, an exception would be when a trusted friend needs you. You might go then on the basis of your relationship. But otherwise it's rarely a good idea to go out blindly in the middle of the night to an unknown situation.

When you're not sure

Sometimes the call doesn't fit neatly into any of the above categories. Maybe someone seems inordinately worried about a situation, and you feel the person is becoming overly desperate. Somehow the caller seems to have lost perspective. In these cases, try to do a long telephone assessment. Many perceived crises can be dealt with on the phone.

Here is an example. Chuck's phone rang at 11:30 p.m. The caller was Wendy. Chuck was scheduled to perform Wendy and Bob's wedding a week from Saturday.

Wendy was crying so hard Chuck could hardly understand her words. "Bob and I had a fight. Everything's over! It's all my fault."

"Take a deep breath, Wendy," Chuck said. "You don't have to rush this." He waited until her breathing had slowed down and her sobs quieted. "Now tell me what it was about."

Chuck listened and commented supportively as Wendy's story came out. After a few minutes, he realized they were both stressed by the wedding preparations and had used the blowup to relieve their tensions.

When the story was finally over, Chuck said, "Do you think Bob still loves you?"

Wendy hesitated a moment. "Yes, but he's really angry."

"Do you love him?"

"Yes. I feel so stupid, fighting like this."

"Well, do you think you can call him and get him to come into my office with you tomorrow?" Chuck asked.

"Probably. He knows we have to do *something.*"

"Good. Things always look their worst at night. Get ready for bed, try to get some sleep, and we'll deal with everything tomorrow. Call in the morning and let me know what time you can both make it. Do you think you can do that?"

She paused again, then sighed. "Yes. Look, this whole thing is such a mess. I'm really sorry I called so late, I just had to talk to somebody."

"No problem," Chuck said. "It's important to deal with this before the wedding. You want to go into your marriage feeling that any potential problems can be handled."

"Yes, you're sure right about that. Okay, I'll call you in the morning. And thanks." She hung up.

Chuck could have rushed right out to see Wendy, but without Bob there, nothing could have been resolved. What she needed was to calm down and give herself time to get a perspective on the situation. Chuck helped her do this by making a later appointment to deal directly with the problem.

When you receive a late-night call that isn't an emergency situation, there are several things you can do to build a correct picture of what's going on.

First, you'll want to find out where the person is, and if he or she is alone. Get the phone number. You may want to ask if the person has been drinking or has taken any medication.

Once you know this information, you will need to depend on your intuition to assess how serious things are. Listen to tone of voice, and try to absorb the person's picture of the crisis. Allow the person to vent. Try to guide him or her through a plan for the rest of the night. Once this is accomplished, make a next-day appointment. Depending on the situation, you may want to have prayer over the phone.

With these kinds of personal crisis calls, the only thing to do is go with your gut—though before this you need to do your best to prepare your gut through proper study and training. Some of us are good at going with our gut, and some aren't. Generally, if you are so worried that you know you won't be able to sleep after a call, you probably need to get up and go.

Chronic callers

Chronic callers fall under two general headings. The first is the lonely person who feels loneliest late at night and calls you for comfort and company. You need to decide what form your ministry should take here. Talk or listen as long as you feel you need to, but end the conversation by trying to help the person make a plan to alleviate the lonely times. Make an appointment to see the person in daytime, when things look brighter and she or he may feel more in charge.

The second type of chronic caller is the complainer. Complainers often mean well, but their calls are negative. They call to complain about you, about others, or about the church. They often call just at bedtime, or maybe a little later. Sometimes they call extremely early, around four or five in the morning.

What can you do about these calls?

First of all, don't take their complaints over the phone. It will guarantee you a bad night's sleep (or no sleep!). Tell them you can't talk right now, but will be glad to hear what they have to say in your office. Then make an appointment. Whatever they have to say will keep, and you really can't deal effectively with complaints over the telephone. You'll want to be alert and awake to really hear what these people are saying and to decide how to respond. Be gentle and warm, but do be firm about not discussing things until the next day.

Why not go every time?

Of course, some clergy feel they should go out each time they're called. That is their decision and may work fine for them. But others of us have discovered a number of valid reasons *not* to go.

First, clergy should never meet members of the opposite sex alone, especially at night. Meet them in a public place or take a friend or a spouse along.

It's also dangerous to meet alone with persons who have a weapon and are threatening to harm themselves or others. Again, try to meet them in the local emergency room. Insist they leave the weapon behind.

Of course, there are less dramatic reasons to put off seeing people in their perceived crises. Many pastors have found that people's problems often look worse at night, when they don't think as clearly. Because of this, a pastor may not really be of practical help until later.

The other main reason many pastors wait a while before going to help someone cope with an emotional problem is that they don't want to be a rescuer. They know it is easy—but not healthy or helpful—to solve someone else's problem.

Why we go

Just as there are reasons not to always rush out when called, there are reasons we do need to respond immediately to each call we receive. They are reasons of ministry—to comfort the bereaved, and to provide spiritual and emotional support in times of crisis.

It finally is up to each of us to decide how best to minister to those who call us for help. When the call comes at midnight, it's good to have given it some thought at noon.

7

Staying Out of Trouble, and Other People's Beds

Sounds pretty juicy, doesn't it? It also sounds easy. You just don't involve yourself sexually with your church members, nor with anyone other than your spouse.

But it isn't that easy. Your job is to love people, all people, even the most attractive ones. So you begin to love them, and you find your love is changing from *philos* (brother/sister love) to *eros* (physical, erotic love). It's not that you plan this, or even want it (though there are troubled pastors, mostly men, who do deliberately and tragically exploit congregational members). Sometimes it just sneaks up on you.

Dan was counseling a young woman in his office one evening after a trustees' meeting. They'd set up an earlier counseling session, but her plans changed and she wasn't able to make it. Rather than put off the session till another time, they agreed to get together after the meeting.

Dan didn't like the authoritarian position of sitting behind a desk when he was talking with people. So he sat beside the young woman on the office couch, leaned back, and prepared to listen.

Her marriage was in trouble. Her husband didn't seem to care about her needs or wants. She felt helpless to do anything about it. A lot of bitterness had built up, and Dan listened responsively as she gave the history of her marriage. After more than an hour of doing little more than nodding, he was caught off guard when she suddenly stopped.

"You're really listening to me," she said. "My husband has never listened to me like that."

She began crying silently, her head bowed and shoulders shaking. Dan reached over to pat her back. She slipped off the couch and knelt at his feet, her head in his lap. She continued to cry, clutching his legs.

Dan was stuck. How could he get this woman to let go of him? On the other hand, she was attractive. The sensations she was rousing had nothing to do with the counseling situation. She needed him, needed someone to hold her, to reassure her. He reached down to raise her off her knees. She slid into his arms, ending up with her head resting on his shoulder, her body leaning against his.

Dan had begun to violate this woman. But he was not eager to quit.

Where did he go wrong?

Of course, we can point to the more obvious mistakes. The first is counseling a member of the opposite sex in an empty church. The second is sitting next to the member. A professional counselor faces a client. The third is deciding to comfort a counselee through touch. The fourth is that Dan apparently didn't recognize that as pastor he was in a position of power over this woman and was therefore responsible to retain professional boundaries at all times.

Touching isn't helping

Look at it this way. Ethical psychologists and psychiatrists don't violate their patients' physical boundaries. They help them, comfort them, teach them how to handle their problems, and develop a relationship which involves a high level of trust. But they do not offer inappropriate physical comfort. If they do, something is wrong. The relationship may have moved into an inappropriate arena.

Pastors often get confused over this issue. We like to think of ourselves as friendly, people-loving souls. Along with our friendliness often comes a tendency to show it in physical demonstrations of affection, such as hugs.

Most clergy know exactly what they intend when they touch or hug a parishioner, but often the parishioner doesn't. And sometimes pastors find out that what they intended became something more with repetition.

What we're saying here is simple. Hug parishioners only in public. Make the hugs very brief. Touch only the back of the huggee's shoulders with your hands. Make it a non-frontal contact hug. Be quite sure the hug is acceptable to the parishioner *before* it is offered.

These rules may seem silly. After all, your job is to love people, to let all people know they are acceptable to God. Some of those folks are hurting and you feel they need more than a quick public embrace to feel cared for. Wrong. It is not your job to be the physical comforter of lonely people. Any comfort given in that manner is temporary and personal. Rather, it is your job to direct them to God so that they may feel God's hand on their spirits. They don't need your physical touch; they need God's spiritual touch.

How not to fall in love

So what do you do if you find yourself infatuated, or even in love, and you fear the situation could become adulterous? The Scripture says if a member of your body offends you, cut it off. But don't panic; that's not your only option. There are steps prior to the final one which work fairly well.

1. Don't tell that person of your feelings. He or she may feel they must reject you and will cut off all or most contact. Or maybe your "love" will be accepted— in which case your problem is compounded. The person also may tell others of your conversation, especially if she rejects you. In either case—acceptance or whispered-about rejection—your Christian witness and career are damaged.

2. Don't tell anyone else your feelings. Talking about them may reinforce them. And your confidante may not keep your secret. The only exception to this rule is that you can and should tell a professional Christian counselor or a trusted ministerial colleague you know will keep confidence and will counsel you strongly against sinning.

3. Avoid being with the person, unless in a large group. You may have to go to some lengths to achieve this, but it must be done. Don't expose yourself to temptation. Try to avoid the person's glance; make little eye contact.

4. Avoid daydreaming about the person. If you find yourself in a daydream or fantasy, stop. Distract yourself, substitute another image, perhaps that of a wall being drawn across the scene to block it out. Infatuation is made up chiefly of hormones and imagination. You can't do much about the hormones. But you can and must control your imagination.

5. Do not believe you will always feel this way. Infatuation is a biochemical reaction. Without renewed stimulation, it fades. This may take a while, but if neglected, the feelings *will* go way.

6. If you find yourself unable to follow the above advice, move. Ask for a new church, one too far away to make it manageable to maintain the relationship. It will be painful and will entail a great deal of trouble, but it is preferable to ruining your life, your family, possibly another family, and betraying your calling.

What if it's true love?

What if you really are in the grip of deathless, hopeless love? If neither of you is married, there is an outside chance you can legitimately proceed. However, this is quite tricky. As pastor, you hold more power than the congregational member. It may be impossible for the two of you to become genuine equals and for the member to be sure the feelings are not in some way the result of your power.

If you are married, you have no choice. You cannot ethically reach out in violation of your own marriage to also violate your pastoral relationship with a congregational member.

Of course, all the above is easy to say and hard to do. When we feel attracted to someone, our culture makes it seem rational to consummate the relationship. To resist temptation feels like denying ourselves. And it is.

But we have to deny ourselves. If we don't, we deny Christ. We can't say this in strong enough terms. An adulterous relationship will destroy marriage, career, loved ones, and a vital part of yourself.

You've already done it

You didn't actually make a decision, you just went along with a situation, not stopping, until it got out of hand. And at the time, it may have felt great. You may even have prolonged the affair. You may still be involved in it. What now?

It's time for those two biblical terms, confession and repentance. And by confession, we don't mean tell your spouse. At least not at first.

Be honest with yourself

You first must confess to yourself that what you have done or are doing is wrong. It's a sin. No two ways about it. Ask God to help you see the truth of this. Then take it in. Believe it.

You will likely need a Christian therapist or counselor to help you accept the fact that what you are doing is actually wrong. After all, most people get into affairs because they feel so *right*. How can love be wrong?

If you've been in the ministry long, you've seen how destructive extramarital affairs are to those who commit them, and to the families they affect. Sooner or later, an affair results in the major destruction of someone, either the participants in the affair or a member of their families. It certainly destroys the trust base of the marital relationship, and once that's gone, it may not be recoverable.

How can anything which results in so much hurt for so many people be right? It can't.

So what do we mean by confession?

1. Confess to God and to yourself that the affair is sin. It is hurting people. It is deceiving people. It is eroding a marital foundation. It is breaking the marriage vows made to God.

2. Confess to a counselor what has happened. Let the counselor help you work out how this came about. Find out what you really feel and think.

3. Confess to your spouse only if you and the counselor agree it will not destroy her or him. Confession may be crucial. Or it may be destructive. Only with a counselor's help can you sort this out.

4. If the affair was with a congregational member, make amends. Each case will differ, but you may be caught in a web of sin which is destroying another person, the person's family, your congregation. You will probably need to confess to your denominational supervisor and accept the consequences as determined by your denomination. Your supervisor may be the right person to help you disentangle the web you have woven around yourself and others.

Decide to quit sinning

Here's where repentance comes in. Jesus said to the adulterous woman, "Go, and sin no more." You have to confess, then repent. Be sorry. Decide you will not continue or repeat the affair.

Is this tough? For some, it will be tougher than confessing they were wrong in the first place. Some people are just more susceptible to sexual temptation than others. And a powerful sex drive is difficult to control. How do you do it?

1. Decide you really want to live without this sin in your life. Until you at least desire to be free of it, you won't be.

2. Go to a therapist and find out what need in your life the affair is attempting to fill. Find out why you are tempted. Where does this feeling have its roots? What is wrong in your marriage that leaves room for this type of intense outside involvement?

3. Work on what you discover. Deal with past issues. Work harder in your marriage. Do whatever it takes to fix the issues that first led to the affair.

4. Make a covenant with yourself and with God. Do this when you can do it honestly. Covenant that you will "sin no more" in this way. Use a concrete symbol during the covenant, something you can put on your keychain or desk to remind yourself of your promise.

5. Be open to God's healing grace. Be willing to accept it. Seek it. This may mean going on retreat. Whatever it takes, let yourself be open to it. If you're truly sorry, God will be truly gracious. Your sin is not unforgiveable—you're not that special. Be humble and accepting of God's forgiveness.

6. If you feel the old temptation returning, flee. Reread the first part of this chapter. Move. Do whatever it takes not to become ensnared again.

We hope you're not reading this with pain. But sadly sin always causes pain. And it doesn't take much experience to know that sin can be hard to recognize when first encountered. If sin weren't so well-disguised, it would be much easier to resist.

8

Can I Tell You a Secret?

Dana had been counseling Ron for six weeks. She was only beginning to discover the depth of his anger toward his wife and the extremes of his moods. She knew that, as his pastor, she needed to refer him to another counselor who had the time and professional expertise to deal with a potentially violent personality.

During their seventh counseling session, Ron seemed more relaxed than usual. Dana commented on it.

"Yes," Ron said, "I *am* feeling better. That's because I've finally decided to take some action."

"What's that?" Dana asked.

"I'm not going to put up with Natalie's stuff any longer. She gives me any more of that garbage about how she's not sure she loves me or I love her or what I'm talking about makes sense—and I'll let her have it."

Dana was confused. Ron had been complaining about Natalie's dissatisfaction in the marriage. Ron was very controlling of Natalie, and she was in a period of mild revolt. He'd been conciliatory, though angry, but now his attitude seemed to have changed.

"What do you mean, you'll 'let her have it?' "

Ron nodded. "Just that. I'll shut her up. A man with a gun doesn't have to put up with that kind of crap."

"You're saying you'll shoot her?" Dana was horrified but tried to appear calm.

"I'm not saying I will and I'm not saying I won't." He spread his hands. "But it's there, the gun's there."

"Ron, do you know what the results would be?" Dana asked quietly. "We're talking prison. The rest of your life would be ruined."

He shook his head. "I know all that. They wouldn't necessarily find a body. There'd be no way to pin it on me, you can be sure of that. You're the only one I've said anything to, and I know you can't tell anyone because you're a preacher, right? Like a priest?"

"I'd have to warn Natalie. It's my duty."

"But you wouldn't tell the police, right?" He looked directly at her. Suddenly Dana wondered if she too was in danger.

What's the answer here? How far does confidentiality go? What is our responsibility as pastors, representatives of God's kingdom, and as citizens being informed of a potential murder? Does our silence make us faithful counselors or accessories to crime?

Two views of pastors as counselors

Most pastors and laypeople subscribe to one of two ways of viewing pastoral confidentiality.

The first philosophy says that people who go to a pastor with a confidence are going to God. If you go along with this philosophy, then all confidences are absolute secrets. You won't break this confidence for any reason, even including murder or the sexual abuse of a child. The closest you would come to revealing your knowledge would be to warn victims obliquely, try to remove them from harm without making clear what you are doing, or try to help others discover the situation through means other than your private information.

If you are of the second philosophy, you let people know they can't count on your silence if they intend to do harm or have already harmed someone. You let them know they are not in a confessional. You will not keep secrets which are dangerous to others. Of course, with this philosophy, it's not likely people will tell you damaging information.

In adopting either philosophy, you have to realize the cost of your stand. In the first, you are willing to be jailed for contempt of court for not testifying in a trial. Although it's not likely, you could even be convicted of being an accessory to a crime. It is a violation of most state laws if you don't report a case where a child is being abused, either physically or sexually. You need to realize that people may come to harm because of your silence.

If you adopt the second philosophy, you are making a different kind of statement about the trustworthiness of clergy. If situations come up where individuals you have counseled feel their trust has been violated, they may never trust clergy again. They may find it difficult to trust anyone. It is also possible that your congregation and community may reduce their trust level of the clergy and of you in particular.

This is a hard issue to deal with. If you haven't yet decided your philosophy, your state laws may help. They may contain definitions of confidentiality. However, some clergy claim these laws don't pertain to them since clergy are dealing with a higher kingdom. These clergy feel they are protected by the separation of church and state.

More common issues

Happily, most of us won't have to struggle with the situation of potential murder. However, there are more common issues which can easily trip us up, unless we have thought out our responses ahead of time.

What *is* true confidentiality?

1. You don't tell your spouse. Frankly, most spouses don't want to know. It makes it difficult for them to see and deal with church people in a normal way if they know secrets about them. Do your spouse a favor. Tell nothing.

2. You don't tell other pastors. It's tempting to ask what they would do, but some pastors are notorious gossipers. Sad, but true. Seems an odd thing to point out in this chapter, doesn't it?

3. You don't tell prayer groups. Many people want the pastor to "share concerns." Unfortunately, these prayer times often turn into gossip sessions. This is especially tricky with medical information. The best way to know whether to share medical reports is to ask the ill persons. They will tell you whether sharing is acceptable or whether they want their privacy guarded. If in doubt, don't say anything about anyone. People may be miffed at you, but they will respect your integrity.

4. You do tell your own therapist, but keep the identity of the individuals you are discussing anonymous. You only tell your therapist if you need consultation, or if you are having personal trouble dealing with the issue.

You may want to take the stand of telling counselees, "I don't keep secrets, and I don't tell them." This means that while you won't reveal another's secret, you will bring pressure on them to reveal it themselves, if that is what is necessary to resolve a problem.

If someone wants you to keep potentially damaging secrets, you stop counseling them. An example of this situation is if a woman in co-counseling with her husband is having an affair which she wants you to keep secret from her husband. In this case you may refuse to see her anymore in a counseling situation until she has a plan to clear up the situation.

Counseling church members is a sticky situation. Many pastors feel it is their duty to serve their congregation in this capacity. Such pastors need special training and certification as pastoral counselors, so they can be sure they are not doing harm. Pastors who offer counseling often find they see several people every week and invest a great deal of time in this capacity.

On the other hand, many pastors feel their other pastoral duties are more vital. They refer all cases which are immediately serious, or require more than two or three sessions, to mental health professionals.

One thing we all find is that the longer we're in a

church, the more difficult it is to keep confidences. We learn many murky facts about people. We know more than we ever wanted to. For a pastor, a bad memory can be a real blessing.

9

They're Trying to Suck You Dry; Are You Providing the Straws?

The phone rang just as Marge and her children were sitting down to supper. Marge hurried to get it, hoping it was a wrong number and she'd be able to enjoy a hot dinner for once.

Her teenage daughters had made the meal and had it ready when she got home from the church. She was pleased that they were doing so well at taking responsibility, and it made things a lot easier for her, since she seldom had an evening at home any more. She did miss cooking though and the relaxation it had always provided.

She lifted the phone. "Hello?" a scratchy voice shouted into her ear. It was Mrs. Philpot, known throughout the community as Crazy Jean. She'd been admitted to the state hospital for observation after she'd gone to her son's house one night, barefoot and furious because she believed she'd seen one of her grandchildren staring in her windows.

Mrs. Philpot was a marginal churchgoer, but a member, so Marge had discussed her obvious paranoia with the woman's family long before the window incident. At that time they had seemed content to leave things as they were. However, after the alleged window-peeping, the son had asked for Marge's help in working out the commitment papers for a five-day evaluation in the state mental hospital.

Marge had obliged with her usual thoroughness. She had consulted an attorney, made the hospital appointment, and helped the woman pack. Since the son worked the day shift at the local battery factory, Marge drove her to the hospital, sixty miles away. The five days were now up.

"Where are you?" demanded Mrs. Philpot so loudly that Marge's daughters looked up from the table. "Do you expect me to stay here all night?"

Marge hesitated. "Why, I thought your son had agreed to pick you up. That was how we left it last week."

"I don't want him. I told him I don't want to see him or any of them ingrates. You brought me here, you take me home. Now!" She hung up.

Marge started to dial the son, then paused. No, his mother had refused his help. If he drove over to get her, she was fully capable of refusing to go with him.

She replaced the phone and sighed. "I have to get Mrs. Philpot," she said.

"But, Mom, you said we'd go to the new movie. We've been looking forward to it all week," her younger daughter said. The older one just looked down at the tablecloth and bit her lip.

Marge felt the frustration building. "Look, I'm sorry," she said sharply. "I really don't have any choice. Maybe we can do the movie next week."

"But it'll be off by then," the girl protested.

"I said I don't have any choice," Marge snapped. "Do you think I want to do this?" She grabbed her purse from the kitchen counter, where she'd dropped it when she got home, and hurried out. "I don't know when I'll be back," she shouted as she let herself out the front door.

Did Marge have a choice? Of course. She could have called the son and told him she couldn't pick up his mother, she had other plans. And what if the mother refused to go with him? That wasn't Marge's problem. It belonged to the woman, her son, and probably the hospital. But someone at the hospital would have been able to take care of it if the son could not.

Marge had taken possession of other people's problems. She had gone from being a helper to being a rescuer. She rescued the son when he wanted help to commit his mother. Rather than walk him through it, she took over and did the work herself, even missing a day of her own work rather than cause him to miss a day of his. When the woman needed to be picked up, Marge again assumed that it was her problem. She would have to rescue the woman from the hospital and the son from the hassle of getting her home.

The above story is an example of what family therapists call *triangling*. Triangling takes place when two parties are having a problem and they draw a third party into the conflict to shift the burden of responsibility for the problem away from themselves.

Pastors often get caught in triangling. After all, it is our job to help people with their problems. As pastors, we know we're to be servants, to carry a burden two miles, to give up our coat and our shirt also.

But when does servanthood become crippling? When does helping them hurt us? And when does our help actually hurt them?

The answers are probably slightly different for each of us, depending on our level of tolerance and other obligations. And there may be some of us whose problem is a laziness or lethargy that *is* in fact preventing our working as hard as we should. For the many of us who tend to work too hard, however, there are a few rules to go by, signposts to warn us that we're doing more than we should and allowing our help to turn into hurting.

Here are the warning signs.

1. You do not really want to help, but you feel trapped, as if there is nothing you can do about it.

If you feel *compelled* to help, stop. Ask these questions. What will happen if I don't help? Will the problem be resolved anyway? Is it vitally important that I help resolve it? Be realistic.

2. You automatically assume the work is yours to do because someone seems to expect it of you.

Is this *really* your obligation as a pastor? Is it more likely someone else's obligation? Who owns the problem? Can someone else take care of it as well or better than you?

3. You realize your own family and perhaps your work

is suffering because of extra demands on your time and energy.

Prioritize what is most important to you. If drop-in counseling has become a problem, insist that people make appointments. Be too busy to see them otherwise. If people expect you to be the general go-for around church—picking up office supplies, choosing Sunday school material, re-tarring the church roof every summer—stop. Look rationally at who really owns those responsibilities, such as teachers, trustees, custodians, and insist they fulfill their responsibilities.

4. You are afraid people will not like you if you deny their requests or disappoint their expectations.

That may happen. But your job is not to be liked. Your job is to be a spiritual leader and to assist the laity in developing their own ministries. They will not dislike you for knowing your job and your own priorities. They may resent having to share the burden, but after all, that is what a church is about. It is not a one-person show. You need to teach them that.

5. You are afraid if you don't do it, it won't get done.

It may not. But will that really be such a tragedy? People learn from their mistakes. If you allow members to make a few mistakes, they will see what happened and ensure that it doesn't happen again. Don't accept blame if it wasn't your job in the first place. Know you are not responsible for seeing that everyone else fulfills *their* jobs. You cannot be everyone's parent.

6. You feel that since you are paid staff, you should do most of the work.

This is small-time thinking. If one person can really do most of the work, not much worthwhile work is getting done. And you are denying other people the chance to serve. Remember, people begin to take ownership when they get involved. If you do everything for them, they'll never take much ownership. They won't really care because, after all, it's your program, or repair work, or whatever—not theirs.

7. It is easy to understand all the above statements, but I still feel compelled to work eighty hours every week. I feel guilty if I don't fulfill every expectation. I cannot even take days off without feeling I really should be working. I rarely take a vacation. I feel driven.

Your problem goes deeper than wanting to do a good job. For some reason your life has become a never-ending treadmill, with enjoyment of living low on your list of priorities. You may be on the way to having a neglected family, decreasing self-esteem, and a heart attack at a young age. Please get into counseling to explore this situation. What is work substituting for in your life? Find out what is going on. Regain control.

Along with counseling, do a reality check. Management experts tell us that people are more productive when they take breaks and have time off from work. What makes you think you are the one exception to that rule?

One more thing—workaholism is not a virtue. Repeat that out loud. The Protestant work ethic is not God's law. You won't get any stars in your crown for running like a hamster on a treadmill.

As pastors, we are often called on to do more than our share. That is fine as long as we are in control of the choice. Sometimes we care so much about a certain program that we will carry it all by ourselves. There is no real problem with that as long as it doesn't become our pattern of ministry.

One thing we need to remember about making superhuman efforts to accomplish huge amounts of work is that it is addictive—both for us and for the people who expect it of us. The more we do for people, the more they want us to do for them. This is a fact. We find that we can never really do enough, can never finally satisfy them or ourselves.

If we try to keep up with ever-increasing demands, or to sustain our output under unreasonably heavy work loads and responsibilities, no one will thank us for it. Rather, they will probably assume we like things that way.

What *will* happen is that we will become caught in a nonending downward spiral, ending with an overwhelming amount of busywork blocking the real work of our ministry. We will become so exhausted mentally and emotionally, so drained of energy, that we have nothing left to offer spiritually. We are talking about, finally, a noneffective ministry—burnout. We do it to ourselves. We provide the straws by which we are sucked dry.

10

R and R: It Doesn't Stand For Railroad

John—husband, father of three, pastor in a growing suburban church—hasn't taken a vacation in two years. He is proud of this. He also doesn't mind telling people that he frequently doesn't take his day off.

There is always plenty of work to do. If it isn't visiting, meeting with committees, or designing worship services, it's planning, reading, or hunting for sermon illustrations. John likes to say the pastor's position is a twenty-four-hour-a-day job.

Although Friday is his official day off—the one he often doesn't take—Saturday is just another work day for John. On Saturday he goes to the office at the church, or retires to the den at home and works on the sermon. All day. Of course, on Saturday night he must get plenty of rest for Sunday, so he and his wife never plan anything but an early evening.

On the evenings of John's workdays, he usually has a meeting scheduled, but even if he has a rare empty evening, he still feels on duty. If his wife suggests they go out for dinner, to a movie, or to visit relatives, he says, "This isn't my day off," and they don't go.

What message is John's wife receiving about her importance in his life? What messages are his children receiving about their place in his priorities?

A pastor owes the church a full work week. For a pastor, work includes such activities as meetings, Bible studies, prayer groups, worship preparation time, visiting, correspondence, counseling, funerals, weddings, and the actual Sunday worship. In most salaried positions, workers are expected to put in somewhat more than forty hours, perhaps up to fifty, and this is a reasonable expectation for pastors.

But after putting in forty to fifty hours a week, a pastor has largely fulfilled most full-time expectations. Additional work is a form of charitable giving. Certainly many of us put in over fifty hours a week, but is this always wise? Is it always helpful? Is it really a good use of time to put most of our extra hours into our work rather than into personal renewal or time with our families?

Taking your day off

Jeanine teaches a church administration course at a major seminary in the south. Each year she assigns a final class project in which each student is to design a year's program calendar. They must fill out the calendar completely, including all preliminary meetings, luncheons, and planning sessions, as well as the program times themselves. They also must include at least one day off each week, and at least two weeks of personal vacation. If they don't put their scheduled days off into their calendar, they don't pass the class.

Jeanine has learned that an enthused pastor with a real drive and love for ministry can easily turn into a workaholic. By making her students schedule their time off, she reinforces the importance of taking time for oneself. She hopes she is turning out pastors who won't burn out within a few years, but who will know how to pace themselves. She also verbally stresses the "day of rest" as laid down in the law of Moses. It helps with her more martyr-oriented and caretaker-type students.

Setting your day off

Once you're committed to faithfully taking time off every week, how do you decide what the best time is? It's a good idea to take your day off each week at a time you can enjoy it. Often it's better not to take Monday off. Many pastors do, because preaching exhausts them, and they want to rest and recover. The problem with this schedule is that they are always worn out on their day off and don't get to enjoy it.

A schedule that works for many pastors is to go to work on Monday. They slowly slide back into the routine, regain their energy, then take a day off later, maybe Thursday or Friday. They try to enjoy their day off and don't even phone the office. Their mind is on vacation status. When Saturday comes around, they may use it as a catch-up day, but often not. After all, the rest of the working population gets two days off a week. Pastors work on Sundays, and each week there are evenings we are at meetings or out visiting.

Provided we are maintaining all our legitimate commitments, we shouldn't feel guilty about taking more than one day off during a week. Like everyone else, we need that time away from work to recharge and be more effective when we do return. If we don't take enough time off, we're cheating not only ourselves but the church.

Of course, there are some weeks in which there is so much pressing work we don't get a real day off. Maybe there's a funeral or a wedding that takes up extra time. Certainly Advent and Lent are packed with extra church activities and less available personal time for the pastor. Is it okay to snatch an afternoon or morning here and there, unscheduled time off, but really the only time available?

Yes. It is not only okay, but probably necessary to give you the energy to do your job well.

The twelve-hour turnaround

Deborah, pastor in a medium-sized inner city church, often found herself worn out in the middle of the week. Friday was her day off, but her church liked Sunday, Monday, and Tuesday evening meetings, so by Wednesday she was usually exhausted. And she still had the Wednesday evening Bible study to prepare for and teach.

After many months of this heavy schedule, she came into the office one Wednesday morning at 8:30, her usual time, and realized she'd left the church only ten hours before. She also realized this had been true of the previous two days. Except for Fridays and Saturdays, she only got one uninterrupted twelve-hour period at home per week, and that was usually Thursday night, the night before her day off.

Deborah was appalled. No wonder her children were complaining that she just ran in for supper and ran back out. Her husband, though supportive, had been feeling neglected lately too—she knew all the signs. And she had to admit she was feeling wiped out much of the time.

That was when Deborah invented the twelve-hour turnaround. Now, during weeks when she simply has too many late evenings and is overstressed, she gives herself a twelve-hour break at least once during the week. That means that if she is at church until 9:30 on Monday night, she doesn't go in until 9:30 on Tuesday morning.

She doesn't use this twelve-hour turnaround every week, but she does give herself permission to use it when feeling stressed. Her main indication of stress is when she cannot recall her schedule for the next day. Usually she can keep two or three days' work in mind. But when she simply can't remember what's coming up the next day, she knows she needs a break. And she tries to take it.

Family evenings

Many pastors have found that their families' needs can often be swallowed up in the never-ending load of church work. It's hard to keep a marriage and family together on only one day of communing time per week. If possible, reserve one evening a week to be devoted totally to your family. This should be in addition to the evening of your day off.

If you're in a church where regularly scheduled meetings or services are scheduled every night of the week, work to change that. Remember, meeting times are mostly arbitrary. They can be changed.

Rick is a pastor who has made Thursday his family night. In his church, there are usually no meetings scheduled for that night. If there are, he lets the chair know that he is unavailable on that date. He doesn't explain nor apologize (though there would be nothing wrong with modeling the importance of family by noting the commitment to reserve a family night).

During these family evenings, the entire family joins in some activity. It may be making a pizza, or playing a board game, or going bowling. Whatever they do, it is something they can all participate in.

Vacations

The most important thing we can say about vacations is this: Take them. Take as many weeks as allowed. Every year.

We all know pastors who take only half of their allotted vacation time or none at all. Many of these pastors have convinced themselves they are indispensable to the church, that it couldn't survive one week without them at the helm. They've usually been encouraged in this thinking by misguided lay people. This is unhealthy thinking. Ask any mental health professional.

Try to set your vacation time well in advance. Include your entire family in making the plans. After all, planning a vacation is half the fun. Talk about it regularly, and keep brochures and pictures on hand. If you can't afford to spend much money, visit friends or relatives. Above all, try to leave town. If you stay around, you may be tempted to work.

Speaking of work, don't take any on vacation. Take a complete break. Don't bring church-related reading materials. Don't attend a church seminar and call it vacation. Don't plan sermons or other church programs while on vacation. Concentrate on your family and yourself. Have fun. Lighten up.

Above all, don't let anyone make you feel guilty about taking your vacation. This time is necessary to refresh and renew your commitment. To skip vacation is like skipping a night's sleep. Your attitude, health, family, and ultimately the church will suffer.

Be in charge of your own calendar

To implement the above advice, you must be in charge of your own calendar and schedule.

Some pastors go into churches where a head of a committee hands them a sheet of paper listing church office hours. They are told this is their work schedule. Other pastors aren't handed a rigid schedule but are asked to make one, give it to the proper committee, then adhere to it.

Ministry mostly doesn't work that way. It has no real schedule. Pastors are called in the middle of the night. They get flashes of inspiration at 5:00 a.m. They have meetings that often run as late as 11:00 p.m. They invite prospective members or committee heads over for dinner to talk about the church. They have breakfast and lunch meetings. They may go out of town for several days to attend training sessions or conferences. The schedule changes each week.

Many pastors have found that they are at their

most creative in sermon preparation and planning at odd hours. We know one pastor who does his best work between 5:00 and 11:00 a.m. After 11:00, he can work adequately for another hour or two, but he's been up since 4:00 a.m., so he runs out of steam by 2:00 in the afternoon. He usually needs a nap before going to evening meetings.

Another pastor, senior minister of a large and prestigious church, is a night person. He gets most of his valuable work done between 3:00 and 11:00 p.m. When other people are winding down, he is revving up. But he's useless in the morning. He doesn't even get to the office much before 10:00 a.m., because he was up till midnight or later the night before. He knows, and his secretaries know, that he may as well not be there at all before lunch, because his energy level is practically nil.

Both of these pastors have recognized the times when they are most effective, and they have demonstrated this effectiveness in their work. It may take a lot of convincing to get a committee to understand that not everyone has the same inner clock. But if they see that the appropriate number of hours *are* being accounted for, they will usually not be hard-nosed.

Most laypeople can't figure out what a pastor does all week, so it may be helpful to give them an hourly timetable of a sample week, with all work-related activities clearly defined and counted as working hours. They will be amazed at all there is to do in your job and may wind up with a better understanding of what ministry is.

Giving time to your priorities

The point of this chapter is that you need and deserve time for yourself, and your family needs and deserves time with you. The stresses of your profession make it too easy to give in to everyone else's needs and ignore your own family. It is also too easy to neglect yourself until you are so overburdened you don't know how to get your life back under control.

Earl, older pastor and father of three adult children now in their twenties, gave me some advice when I was just out of seminary.

"If I had anything I could do over," he said, "I'd spend more time with my family. You never get those years back. A family won't run on autopilot. By the time I realized what I'd missed and what I'd neglected, it was too late. Don't make the same mistake."

11

The Five-Years-from-Now Rule

We could have called this chapter "Setting Priorities," but that sounds boring and complicated. Plus it's reminiscent of being told to eat your vegetables. Actually, if you follow the five-years-from-now rule, setting priorities becomes fairly easy. It's following the priorities you set that takes courage.

It works this way. Whenever you have a conflict of proposed activities, or you have to decide between priorities, ask this: Five years from now, what will make a difference? Will it really matter that I did _____? Will it have made any lasting difference?

You'll be surprised how often the answer is no. Busywork tends to fill our schedules, and this rule helps you recognize it. It also helps you recognize truly worthwhile activities.

Marilyn and her husband, Rick, were copastors of a large inner-city church. They had been at the church three years and things were running smoothly. This church held council meetings the first Thursday of every month. Both pastors were expected to be there, and the church even provided childcare for their two grade-school-aged sons during these meetings.

In November, their oldest son, Kevin, brought home a sheet for them to sign, giving him permission to be in the school Christmas play. He was very excited at the prospect of being in a "real play," as he called it.

Marilyn noted that the play would be the first Thursday in December. She decided Kevin could easily go with their neighbors, whose little girl also would be in the play. There wouldn't be any after-school rehearsals, so that wouldn't be a problem. She and Rick signed the permission sheet.

As the time for the play neared, Kevin grew ever more excited. He repeated his lines at breakfast, after school, at supper. His younger brother recited lines with him. By late November, Marilyn and Rick very much wanted to go to the play, and Kevin assumed they would. But the council meeting date was set in stone. No other night could be negotiated, especially not in December, when everyone was so busy.

On the Saturday night before the play, Rick and Marilyn were in the kitchen, pondering options.

"Look, Rick," Marilyn said, "maybe you could go. After all, nothing vital will be going on at this month's meeting. I could cover for us."

He shook his head. "You want to see the play as much as I do. And how would Kevin feel if you couldn't be there? Maybe you should go to the play and I to the meeting."

"The trouble is, this is really important to Kevin," she said. "He'll be hurt if we aren't *both* there."

"Yes," Rick said, "but if we skip the council meeting, that hurts the feelings of the entire church. The chair has already asked for an appointment with both of us on Wednesday to iron out some of the business. It would look as if we were neglecting our jobs."

"I know. What a mess! But I can't bear to disappoint Kevin. This is so important to him. And to me."

Rick shrugged. "What can we do? It's our job to be at the meeting."

Rick and Marilyn agonized. Finally they decided Marilyn would go to the first half of the play, then leave at intermission to join Rick at church. Kevin was disappointed that his dad didn't see him in the play, and that his mother wasn't there to pick him up back-stage afterward, along with all the other mothers.

The five year rule could have saved all their ago-nizing and Kevin's hurt. If they had missed the council meeting, would it have made any difference five years later? Probably not.

On the other hand, would it have made a differ-ence to Kevin five years later? Yes. He would remem-ber being in his first school play for his entire life. It would have been good for him to be able to associate that memory with both his parents being there for him. Instead he would remember waiting backstage with a neighbor's child, watching all the other parents com-ing to pick up their children.

This rule doesn't apply only to our activities with children. It is applicable to any situation in which we find our home life in conflict with our jobs, or in which we have to decide among different job priorities.

Let's say that the weekly Wednesday night prayer meeting falls on your tenth wedding anniversary.

What's more likely to make a difference five years from now—that you went to a weekly prayer meeting, or that you made a special effort to have a romantic anniversary evening? Or you can look at it from the negative side—if you skip one of the above, which will make more difference in the long run? The negative side to the question is often easier to answer.

So what are we saying? That sometimes you have to put your job responsibilities in second place to your family needs? Yes. Sometimes we all have to do that. We're not advocating avoiding legitimate work. But when there is an unavoidable conflict between responsibilities, use the five-year rule and be honest about the probable outcome.

The rule is also applicable to most work situations. If you are needed in two places at once, or you have to decide to commit your energy to one program or another, recite the five-year rule. Five years from now, which action will have been most fruitful? Which one probably will not matter?

The only difficult thing about this rule is following through. It's not easy to explain to the council chair that you cannot be at a council meeting. It's not easy to disappoint people who are counting on you. But we all must make priorities in life and this rule can help guide that process. The rule can save anguish and guilt in decision making, as well as remorse afterward.

The other and best reward for following this rule is that five and even ten years from now, we can look back and be glad we asked ourselves what the probable outcomes would be. We can congratulate ourselves on having had the courage to make some hard choices.

12

Getting a Decent Raise Without Groveling

It's time to set the new budget; your church simply does not have the money to meet it. Rather than challenge the congregation to dig deeper, the committee decides to trim the fat, tighten a few belts. The first belt to be tightened is yours. No raise this year.

Here's another scenario. The church is doing okay financially—not much extra but no real crunch either. You know you've been doing your best, you figure it's time to ask for that merit raise you've been expecting for the last few years. They turn you down. It's nothing personal, they assure you; they just don't see how they can do that with the economy the way it is and all.

One more. Money has never been a real problem in your church. There are some big givers and a foundation and trusteeship, so things are pretty well set. But there's still no chance for a raise much above cost-of-living increases. They've never done it before and are afraid of setting a precedent.

What's wrong with all these churches? Where's their spirit of generosity, their appreciation of a job well done, their personal affection for their spiritual leader?

That last question is the one that hurts. You serve these people, you sit with them through their personal crises, you bury their dead, visit their sick, baptize their children, marry them to their sweethearts, and try to bring God's word to them on a weekly basis. Yet you're lucky to get a 3 percent salary increase and often may get no increase at all. What's going on here?

What's going on is that people love a bargain. This is the same mentality that gives any job to the lowest bidder, no matter the quality of workmanship. If excellent quality is delivered, so much the better—if not, no matter, they got what they paid for.

What also is going on is that when people look at a budget sheet they put on a self-oriented mentality. They try to decide what will hurt *them* the least. Frankly, they don't see your paycheck as having any effect on them. And that is where they make a mistake. They are looking only at today, at what is expedient. They aren't looking down the road, two or three years from now, to see what affect their bargaining will have.

If you have been on the receiving end of a less-than-expected raise, or no raise at all when you felt you deserved one, you already know the effect. It hurts a lot—for a long time.

For although the committee meant nothing personal when they denied you increased compensation, they delivered a very personal message—"we don't care about you or the quality of your life. Your needs and wants are not a priority here. Your career is of no importance to us."

That may not be the message they mean to send. But it is the message you *feel,* no matter how they try to soften it. Your next thought is that perhaps you should go to a church where you will be more appreciated.

Michael had been at his 300-member church for three years. Each year he received a minimal 3 percent cost of living increase. At the end of the third year, he was hoping for more and needed more to meet obligations. Inflation had outstripped his raises. He had been doing a good job, and he knew the congregation was aware of it. He was working on a doctorate and had started a special Bible study in the church centered around the doctorate work, which had been received very well. He was getting many comments on his sermons and his home visits. People were generally quite pleased with his work.

That was why it came as such a shock when the pastor-parish relations committee told him they just could not afford to give him a raise. After all, they were mostly farmers and teachers and did not foresee that their own income would go up significantly, so they did not see how they could raise his income either.

There was no real discussion about the quality of the job he was doing, nor about his expectations. There was no talk of designing a new stewardship campaign or increased giving. There was just a flat consensus. They would hold the line.

Michael went home and told his wife the news. Although they could understand the committee's rationalization, they felt hurt. They began to question their relationships with these people. They felt a coldness in the decision and wondered if it reflected the feelings of the entire church.

Michael's mistake was that he had expected the committee to take care of him. He looked at a raise the same way he had looked at a Christmas gift from his parents when he was a child. If he knew he'd been a good boy, he hoped for that big gift, the bicycle or the electric train. When he just got new clothes and a book, he had to rationalize that it was a gift and he could not really complain about it.

There are two fallacies involved in expecting a committee to take care of you in this way. The committee members are not your parents. And a raise is not a gift.

What is a committee? A group whose purpose is to perform work and make decisions for the good of the entire body.

What is a raise? Fair compensation for services rendered and recognition of the quality of those services.

It is your job to educate the committee as to what *their* job is and what your expectations are, based on standard rates for those services and on the quality you particularly bring to those services. It is not up to you to find the money. It is usually not up to them to find the money either. Another committee takes care of that.

What if the church feels its finances are exhausted? You'll need to do some research to discover if the stewardship levels are really as high as can be expected. If they are, and the money is committed, then you'll have to accept the situation and your present salary. If you find there are resources that haven't been explored, help lead the congregation's stewardship campaign. Help members find ways to increase giving.

Once they feel they are on solid ground again, you can return to the issue of just compensation.

Okay, so how do you do that?

First, committees try to take a businesslike attitude toward the pastor's compensation. Do the same thing. Do your homework.

Find out where your congregation ranks in membership and average attendance among churches of your denomination and geographical region. Then look up the salaries of pastors who serve churches that have attendance and membership averages within fifty persons of your own church's averages, both above and below. Do the same with pastors in your ordination class, ranking your salary with theirs.

If you are in the lower half of the rankings, you can build your case on what is just and fair compensation. Point out you are being undercompensated. Give the committee a salary range that would be acceptable to you. Note that we mention a range, not a figure. Ranges are negotiable, and they give the committee a little freedom. If they still want to deny any raise or provide one which is too small, tell them if you feel it is inadequate.

Now is the time to negotiate. That is what salary talks are about. If committee members understand that you truly care about what you earn, and that it is a reflection of your professional performance, they will look for other ways to adjust the budget. That is, they will if they care about keeping you as a satisfied worker. However, if saving a small percentage of your salary is more important to them than your job satisfaction (when reasonable adjustments *could* be made), it may be time for you to change churches.

What if you are in the middle of the compensation scale or in the upper half? That makes everything more difficult. You must clearly illustrate the quality of leadership and effort you bring to your work. The committee must see that the congregation is getting an obviously superior product for its money. You also must question your motives. Are you already being fairly compensated? If so, back down. The goal is not to push your salary as high as possible. The goal is simply just compensation.

Finally, it may not be a good idea to bring personal need or debts into any discussion. That deflects attention from a professional issue of just compensation to an issue of taking care of the pastor. It encourages them to be parental, rather than businesslike, and puts you in the child's role.

If you cannot come to an agreement, you may both want to bring in an outside arbitrator, someone skilled in negotiations and human resources. Denominational overseers can sometimes help.

Above all, put your ego aside during salary negotiations. Do not take anything personally. Do not become defensive. People get emotional about money. Remember that just as you don't want the committee to become emotionally committed to denying you a raise, you should guard against becoming too emotional about needing a raise.

Most committees look at a salary as simply another item on a budget list. Do the same, as far as you can. After all, you both have the same objectives—fair compensation, a feeling that everyone is satisfied, and the best possible outcome for both parties.

13

Performing Without a Net

Taking risks can be a scary thing. But it beats the alternative—always doing things the same old way guarantees eventual failure. Even the best programs repeated often enough get stale.

Although most pastors realize the truth of this, it can be difficult to persuade a church that growth involves change. After all, change is stressful. It's much easier to stay with the familiar. It's hard to continually face new challenges, try out new programs, and do new kinds of ministry. It may be exciting, but it's work.

Lena found she was in a church that always asked, "How did we do it last year?"

Her church was declining in size as old members died and were not replaced by new ones. The membership had been going down for eight years. Lena knew that the only way to turn that around was to renew the church's vision of its ministry to the local community. This meant new programming, targeted at bringing in new people.

To persuade the church to support new programs,

Lena had to build a new perception for members of why their congregation existed. The longtime members had settled into thinking of it as a place to belong, where the old traditions could be counted on, where they could meet friends and have good fellowship.

In many ways, their picture of the church resembled that of a private club. They liked the idea of taking in new members, but they only wanted to assimilate a few each year. Too many new faces made them anxious. They also thought new programs would be okay, but they wanted to limit them. One every year or two was about right. After all, new programs took a lot of energy.

Lena started by talking about the church in her sermons. She reminded the congregation of what the early church must have been like. She helped them see why those early Christians drew together and what they did in their ministries.

Lena also involved the church council in expanding the church's idea of its ministry. She encouraged the council to establish a long-range task force. The church's vision of ministry was renewed and updated. People with energy were recruited to help with the planning and implementation of new programs. Often they were folks who had never been included in the administration of the church up to that point.

All this took a long time. Lena worked on it for two years before she could really sense a change in the attitude of the congregation at large. And the emerging attitude was one of uneasiness. The members liked to feel they were progressing, but they were uncomfortable with change. There were so many new things being proposed. It all felt so busy. It was unsettling to see increasing numbers of unfamiliar people in the congregation.

As this discomfort surfaced, Lena altered her tactics. She took several small steps to nurture those who were worried. A large-print bulletin was introduced for the older members who had failing eyesight. Special recognition was given to longtime members. A Sunday school class began sponsoring surprise parties to honor its members, using the old *This Is Your Life* format.

Lena found that her role was often that of salesperson. She couldn't do all the programming herself, so she had to sell it to volunteers. She also had to sell the idea that programming was even necessary. "You have to be willing to take risks in order to see results," became her constant refrain.

The church gradually began to see that if they had several programs going, at least half of them would probably be successful. And they liked this success. They began to feel that they were accomplishing good things. They felt like winners, and they came to understand that other people like to be associated with winners. For the first time in a long while, they felt they were a congregation on the move.

Lena's church finally began to see real growth and significant new ministries once its picture of itself had truly changed. The quiet peace of the private club was gone. However, in its place was the excitement of an active, growing group of Christians willing to take risks in order to do ministry.

Lena's church had gone through an uphill struggle.

She was discouraged repeatedly and found herself facing failure time and again in her efforts to get things moving. She often wondered if it was worth it. However, luckily for Lena's church, she had a wide streak of stubbornness. She also felt strongly that God was calling her church to a more vital, effective ministry. Her perseverance finally paid off.

How do you begin to take risks in the church, to lead members up unknown paths, to reach an untapped group of people who might find a church home with your congregation?

It can't be done overnight. In fact, it requires a long-term investment on the part of the pastor. But there are steps that can help you get started.

1. You have to be in a church long enough for people to feel they can trust you. At least the leadership has to feel this way. They need to know you're not leading them toward disaster.

2. Include others in the ownership. Find leaders who have the ability to be visionary. Use the pulpit to bring the issues in front of the congregation. Be open.

3. Work in group process. This way others can also own the risk, the rewards, and possibly the pain. Use the church council, and the missions and evangelism committees. Use anyone who might help.

4. Share your convictions. The pastor has to be able to say, "I feel strongly about this." Use sermons to illustrate active ministry. Preach what you believe; believe what you preach.

5. As you move toward outreach, nurture those who are already in the church. They are the base of your congregation. They need to feel loved and cared for. If their needs are first met, they will then be able to welcome newcomers.

These rules are general, but then, every church is unique. If your church is in an area with a growing population, your job will be easier. People will simply wander in off the streets. All you have to do is figure out how to make them come back.

If your church is in an area with a stable or declining population, the problem is compounded. You can't use new people to help run new programs, because there aren't any. The longtime attenders have to get a fresh image of their place in the church as well as of the church's mission in the local community. Your work is cut out for you.

Of course, you may be reading this and thinking, "My church would never buy that. They like things just the way they are. They'll never change."

This could be the case. You have to realize that, despite all you do, it may not work. Then you have to be secure enough to accept that and go on.

But remember the parable of the talents. We are not called to maintenance. We are called to ministry.

As one risk-taking pastor says, "A pastor will always get flak from the congregation. Better to get flak for doing something than for doing nothing."

14

So You Blew It

Oops. It was bound to happen. And it did. You blew it. You feel embarrassed, and insecure. Why didn't you see it coming? What makes it worse is that everyone else knows, or will soon—you blew it. Well, now they'll realize you're not perfect. How are you going to deal with that and go on?

Admit it

Nothing's worse than someone who has blown it and won't admit it.

Bruce was a youth minister in a large church. He took the youth group on their annual campout and asked a young married couple to go along as extra chaperones.

On the second day of the campout, the group was scheduled to rent canoes and take a trip down the river. However, it had rained heavily the previous week, and the water was up. The chaperone couple counseled against canoeing, but Bruce wanted to go, as did two of the older high school boys.

Bruce left the chaperones with the main group of teenagers, took the two boys with him, and rented one canoe. He arranged to have the canoe outfitter pick them up several miles down the river.

They started out. Although the outfitter had provided life jackets, Bruce didn't put his on, so the boys didn't either.

The water was fast, and the three were having a great time. The current carried them downriver so quickly they didn't need to paddle. Bruce was in the stern. He ruddered to keep them on course, and the two boys hung on as the canoe shot past floating logs and debris washed into the river by the recent rains.

Soon they were near the area where the outfitter had said there were rapids. He'd advised them to get out and portage the canoe to the bottom of the rapids.

Bruce looked around. "No, I think we'll be okay. The water's up so high the rapids should be pretty deep underneath the surface. We'll ride it out."

The boys cheered as they swept round a bend and saw the churning of the rapids ahead. Bruce steered the canoe toward the deepest flow of water. The ride was wild and exciting. The front of the canoe bucked up and down, water splashing into the canoe and just as quickly being tossed back out by the action of the waves. They were almost through the last of the rapids when they began drifting toward a large rock projecting eight feet out of the water.

Bruce ruddered strongly, but the current was too fast. "Paddle, boys!" he yelled. But the water kept moving them toward a depression at the base of the rock, where they could see the swirling of a deep whirlpool.

Finally Bruce knew they were going to hit. "Jump!" he shouted. Both boys bailed out on the left side of the canoe. Bruce felt himself being dumped over. Then the undercurrent had him and he was being pulled roughly through sharp rocks. He was choking when he finally felt sand beneath his feet and was able to stumble to the left river bank.

For a moment he just leaned on the bank, gasping for air, then he remembered the boys. He looked around wildly. Up on the bank above him, he saw the red of a T-shirt. One of the boys had climbed up there to safety. He started up the hill and saw that the other boy was also there, lying a few feet away from the first.

When he got to them, both boys were so frightened they didn't want to talk. One was sobbing, the other shaking as if with a chill.

Bruce looked back at the river. The canoe was lodged at the base of the rock, its open end facing upstream. The water pouring into it was holding it in place, and the force of its flow had bent both ends of the canoe slightly down toward the sides of the rock. The bow was crumpled.

Bruce and the boys walked to their pickup point. The canoe outfitter was furious at the loss of his canoe and insisted that Bruce pay for it. Bruce didn't have the money, so he had the church billed for the canoe.

When the boys' families learned what had happened and that their sons weren't wearing lifejackets, they were outraged. The pastor-congregation relations committee confronted Bruce.

Bruce made excuses and denied errors in judgment. Then he tried to close the discussion, saying,

"Look, it's over. I want to put it behind me."

He was fired. The committee's decision was based not only on his carelessness, but on his lack of responsibility. He wouldn't admit he had made a mistake.

Immediate action

You'll probably never blow it as badly as Bruce did, but when you do fail, what can you do?

1. At your first realization of your error, call a few trusted church members and admit what happened. This will help retain their trust in you.

2. Ask these church members for help and advice. Depend on their wisdom. They will become your allies and will defuse any resulting anger and frustration.

3. Apologize to the proper people or committee. Plead imbecilic behavior. Admit your intentions and your ignorance of the possible outcome. You may need to do this whether you feel it was directly your fault or not.

4. Become defenseless, not defensive. Don't defend your mistake. That blows it out of proportion.

5. Let the committee (or whoever) vent frustration. Take whatever they say and realize you don't need to respond. They'll feel better if they've let you know how they are reacting. Once they've dealt with the incident, they can bring closure to it. They will feel it was resolved. Then the problem will fade rather than be an open wound.

6. Don't let the problem fester and become bigger than

it is. Deal with it immediately. One pastor likes the analogy of a leaky boat. He says that when you've blown it, think of it as knocking a hole in a boat. First you have to control further damage, so the boat doesn't fill up with water. Once you've prevented the damage from spreading, you can fix the hole and keep the boat floating.

7. Assure the congregation it won't happen again. You've confessed, now comes repentance. Let members know you've learned from your mistake.

8. Don't dwell on it. Move on. This was what tripped up Bruce. He wanted to go immediately to the moving-on part without going through the pain of the dealing-with-it part.

Although mistakes are always painful, it helps if you can go through the process with grace and even humor.

Joe was trying to juggle a new study program at his church and needed a weeknight when everyone in the congregation could attend. As pastor, he made an executive decision. He moved choir practice night.

By the next week, he discovered he'd blown it in a big way. Not only was the entire choir furious, the choir director was threatening to quit. He'd caused a minor catastrophe and a major headache.

He did the only thing possible. Choir practice was immediately moved back to its original night, and Joe apologized personally to the choir director, to the choir, and to the church for making such a ridiculous error.

The next week Joe sent out a letter to each choir member, again apologizing. Included with the letter was a drawing of a hot-air balloon. It was upside down and sinking. The caption under the drawing read, "That idea didn't fly very well, did it?" The humor helped with further healing and closure.

Most mistakes can be healed with the appropriate apologies. A pastor must always be willing to admit to being flawed. However, pastors can err so badly they never regain the congregation's trust. Their error can even carry on into the next pastor's tenure, and prevent the automatic trust level that usually goes with accepting someone as a new pastor.

Laura's congregation had to go through this situation. Laura came to her small-town church full of energy and caring. The people loved her and her family.

However, over three years they saw Laura's energy gradually change to passive acceptance of the status quo. She came to meetings with her usual energetic vocabulary, but there seemed to be an artificiality to her responses they hadn't noticed earlier.

When Laura promised to follow up on suggestions and ideas, she never did. She often seemed a little disoriented during evening meetings. At her annual evaluation, she became defensive and lashed out at the group. She then apologized, said she'd had a hard week, and left the room in tears.

People who lived near the church noticed that Laura was spending a lot of time in the office alone late at night. Her husband, previously openly supportive, seemed to become introspective and quiet. Her children grew rowdier and were sometimes almost out of control during Sunday school.

One Sunday Laura wasn't at church. The district superintendent was present. He took the pulpit and announced that Laura had entered a treatment program for alcoholism and would be away from the church for about six weeks. He conveyed her request for their prayers, and suggested they might want to show extra support when she returned.

The church was relieved to find out what the problem was, but many members felt betrayed. They didn't like the idea of a pastor drinking at all. To find she was an alcoholic seemed to them the ultimate disgrace. A few people left the church.

When Laura returned, full of remorse, but also more like her old self, she thought her ministry could pick up where it had left off. However, she soon found that the church had no real trust for her. They were openly supportive and caring, but underneath lurked the assumption that she would probably disappoint them again.

Laura worked hard to reestablish trust but was unable to regain even the baseline level she'd had when she first arrived at that church. She realized her effective ministry there was over. She finally asked for an appointment to another church.

The church she left was sorry to see her go but also relieved. Now they could get on with their own ministry under new leadership. However, the new pastor found that his enthusiasms were greeted with guarded acceptance. He was watched very closely, especially in potentially stressful situations. It took him three years to build a good trust level—about the same period of time trust had been eroding under Laura's pastorate.

It's easy to blow it, and hard to recover. But it happens to each of us again and again. When it happens to you, try to deal with it with humility and humor. Let the wave of other people's frustration roll over you, but don't choke on it. Just keep reminding yourself that you're only human, and God's grace covers all. Surely the congregation has absorbed some of that grace. You hope.

15

A Building Program Without Controversy Is like Noah's Ark Without Fleas

So you're considering putting up a new building, or doing major renovations—pretty exciting stuff. Everyone feels involved. Suddenly everyone has an opinion on literally everything. And they don't agree.

How can you minimize the conflicts? How can you keep this exciting new growth from turning into a monster of debt and regret? How can you keep everyone happy?

You can't keep everyone happy. Forget it. But there is one primary way you can minimize conflicts.

Have everyone agree on the right—perhaps the only—reason they should build. At first the congregation will say it's because the youth program is growing, the community is expanding, or just because the old church is getting too run-down and isn't worth saving.

But if you help members explore in depth why they need new facilities, sooner or later they will come up with the real reason for building: to provide the people of the community with a place to meet God.

It's important to come to this realization early. After all, the new building will be used for generations to come. You want to look that far forward when building. It can help put things in perspective when decisions have to be made.

The people on First Church's renovation committee wish their counterparts in the 1950s had recognized the longevity of their decisions. The First Church sanctuary was completed in 1958. Its design elements had been contemporary at the time and quite novel.

Maybe too novel. No one had been happy with the twelve-foot-high cylindrical pulpit, accessible only by a flight of seven steps. They also hated the giant wooden structure, referred to as "the birdcage," that hung from the ceiling above the choir loft. It had been built to house the organ pipes but was discovered to be too small when the organ was ready was ready to be installed. The organ pipes had to be put into the vacant bell tower, an area not totally weatherproof. This led to a need to replace the organ thirty years later.

The other item the new committee would love to replace, but can't afford to, is the large stained glass window at the back of the sanctuary. Its design was heavily influenced by the artistic style of Pablo Picasso. The youth in the congregation refer to it as the "chicken" window.

The window is supposed to be a contemporary rendering of the descending dove, but everyone agrees it looks more like a monstrous chicken. When the artist first submitted the drawing in 1957, it was rejected. However, something went wrong with communications between the building committee and the artist, and the rejected drawing was made into a stained glass window and delivered to the church. The building committee didn't have the nerve to reject the finished project, so the window was installed.

Today First Church is working on renovations. The current building committee is giving much thought to future generations who will have to live with the current congregation's taste and decisions. The committee is determined not to introduce another item such as the "chicken" window.

Yes, it's easier than you'd imagine to make a gross error, or even several, when you've got a building going up and lots of decisions to be made. How do you ward off such problems as ensnared First Church?

There are several ways to put your mind at ease. Before you call for blueprints, consider the following guidelines, culled from the wisdom of pastors who have successfully guided their churches through building programs.

1. Take your time. The church will first need what one pastor calls a "critical mass"—a majority of people who share the vision. These are the people who will support the program and keep it going, no matter what happens. There's no point beginning to build if you don't have a majority in favor. As pastor, you shouldn't be trying to convince them to start. When the time is right, they'll be telling you they *need* to build.

2. Learn and follow the denominational guidelines. You don't want to reinvent the wheel. Besides, you have to know the rules to qualify for denominational help, advice, and support. This isn't the time to be a Lone Ranger.

3. Form the building committee carefully. Try to include those who may have had this kind of experience in other settings, either at their jobs or other churches. It's also good if you can get an architect, an engineer, and a lawyer on your committee. If you don't have any on the committee, you may need to hire these folks to be your consulting experts during the project.

Be sure both sexes are well-represented on the building committee. They'll have different ways of viewing various stages of the project. Be sure to have a mix of generations and racial groups from within the congregation.

4. Have a clear financial plan. The committee or a task force will need to know how they plan to raise money, how much they will need, and various places they expect to get loans. They also should have a contingency plan to deal with cost overruns—they'll need it.

5. Keep your sense of humor. If members see you're anxious about the building program, they'll become anxious. Be ready to greet problems with laughter rather than wringing of hands. You will help shape congregational attitudes.

6. Inundate the congregation with information. There should be no secrets on the building committee. Communication will keep the congregation informed and involved. Tell members everything—give them so much information they have trouble taking it all in. If they feel the committee is holding anything back, conflicts will arise. They will be especially nervous if they suspect they are being misled about money. Tell them all news, good and bad. They deserve to know as much as the committee knows.

7. Have the building committee come to unanimous agreement on every important decision—no matter how long it takes. If conflicts are not settled in the committee, the committee will promote conflicts in the church at large and people will separate into opposing camps. When you come to a disagreement, take your time. Table the discussion for a week or two. Meet again. If you still disagree, table the issue again. Do this as long as you can, until a compromise is reached. If the committee refuses to let itself be hurried, it can make much wiser and happier decisions.

There's one more important maxim: use professionals in areas where quality of work is vital to the project.

Bert and his rural congregation found out the importance of this last rule when they decided to build a new sanctuary. Wanting the design to be truly their own, they commissioned one of their members, a high school art teacher who did drafting on the side, to come up with blueprints.

The teacher designed a beautiful sanctuary. It was wide, deep, and had a high vaulted ceiling that made it feel even larger than it was. The building committee loved it. However, the church was in the snowbelt. The committee felt that heating all that space between the floor and the ceiling would be a waste of energy. The ceiling was dropped from thirty to fifteen feet, against the teacher's advice. The county didn't have a well-trained building inspector, so the plans were approved, including the lowered ceiling and roof.

The building committee hired a contractor to pour the foundation, and much of the construction work was done by church members. When the building was complete, the sanctuary was indeed wide and had a large seating capacity. But it seemed somewhat squatty and claustrophic inside, because of the low ceiling.

After some initial disappointment, the congregation reconciled itself to the ceiling. Everything was fine until the first big snowfall of the season. Two feet of snow fell on the roof. The only roof support consisted of the outer walls. Six hours after the snow fell, the roof caved in.

There had been a mistake in the calculations of how much weight the walls could hold. The change in the angle of the roof from the original plans had also changed the way the load was distributed. Fortunately the snow fell on a Friday night, and the church was vacant when the roof collapsed Saturday morning.

If Bert and his building committee had hired a professional architect, they would have been informed that their final design had a fatal flaw. They also would have had a better idea of the visual effect of the low ceiling. If they had hired a professional contractor to oversee the building work itself, the contractor might have realized the error and been able to avert the catastrophe. As it was, they had to rebuild and hire an architect to salvage what they could of their damaged building.

This example is extreme, but these things do occasionally happen. Volunteer labor is a wonderful way to get a congregation to take ownership in a building, but you need to know when to hire professionals. It is rarely a waste of money to get the benefit of their education and experience.

Architectural evangelism

All church buildings are different, each reflecting the congregation that attends it. When we are deciding on a church design, we have to consider its many different functions—worship; education; youth center; place of weddings, baptisms, funerals. There are a myriad of designs that will accommodate all these activities.

However, the one constant for any church is that people expect to meet God there. Remember that principle. Remember that you are building the church not only for yourselves but for generations to come. Share these ideas repeatedly with the rest of the congregation. Then your time of building can contain more celebration than conflict.

16

So You've Finally Hit the Big Time

You've finally made it. Big church, big parsonage, big salary, big staff—well, at least *a* staff. The big time. How long till the glamour wears off? A month? Maybe two or three? When the reality of the big time hits, it can hit hard. Big time equals big stress, big responsibility, and the opportunity to fail in a really big way. So how do we cope when the big time hits us?

Will found out early. He was feeling great after completing his first Sunday morning worship services at his new church. There had been over 200 in attendance at the early service, and 500 at the second. He knew he'd given one of his better sermons. He'd also loved preaching to such a large congregation. His last church had averaged about 300 in worship, a good size, but it couldn't compare to the mega-church feeling he got here. This was heady stuff!

He was in his office taking off his robe when a small man knocked on the open door and walked in. He carried a sheet of paper.

"Here, Reverend," the man said, holding out the

sheet. "These are the grammatical and usage errors you made in your sermon during the second service today."

Will smiled, thinking it was a joke. "You kept track?"

The man looked at him without smiling. "I know you came from a small church. You'll find the expectations here are more stringent. We expect our senior pastor to know the King's English and to use it." His expression relaxed. "This was your first Sunday, and of course you were nervous. That probably accounts for many of the errors. However, I do hope you will review the sheet, and have the printed copy corrected before it goes out to the shut-ins."

"I don't make a printed copy," Will said. He felt himself becoming defensive and fought against it. "I don't preach from a manuscript. I use notes, and ad lib on the spot."

"Oh, you will have to have a printed copy. It's expected here, don't you know." The man nodded and backed out. "I hope you find the information helpful. I look forward to next week's sermon."

Will stood at his desk, and stared at the sheet. There were nine errors noted.

Suddenly he felt very tired. Was this kind of thing common in a very large church? Did they expect perfection? Just what were their expectations? He felt his first twinge of anxiety.

Keep track of who you are

A big-time church really is a different animal than its smaller relatives. The expectations for the senior pastor are often beyond what any human can meet. Members expect to get an excellent preacher; a top-drawer manager; a wise counselor; an expert in areas such as finance, programming, evangelism, education, and fundraising. In addition, some congregations want a political activist, a human rights organizer, and a denominational bigwig. They also expect the senior pastor to know each of their names in a month or so.

How do you cope with such an unrealistic job description?

First, keep your head on straight. Keep a realistic perspective of where you are and who you are.

Begin by prioritizing your calendar. You'll find your schedule will be filled like never before, so begin by reserving time for you. If you don't block out time for personal spiritual devotion and for family, it won't be there.

Consider putting in a regular time slot for personal counseling. When you have a major change in your life, such as entering big-time ministry, it's a good idea to get into therapy, even if you can only work it in once a month. Doing therapy is a good self-perception check. Your therapist can be a trusted confidante who helps you sort out what's happening in your life.

The easiest way to cope with awesome expectations is to not think about them much. You know you're not a miracle worker, so don't let others put that burden on you. You certainly should work at improving your skills. And you'll need to do more reading than ever to keep up with things and generate new ideas. But after all, you're just you. Let yourself grow into the job. Don't be afraid to make mistakes.

Managing the groups

Every large church is actually a collection of smaller churches. All of these small churches existing together in one building can lead to chaos if not well managed.

One senior pastor likes to use the analogy of a shopping mall in talking about the large church. The different groups within the church are like the small shops in a mall.

If we carry the analogy further, we see that the pastor is the acting mall manager. It's the manager's job to know which stores are there, which new ones are being planned, which are declining, and what type of specialty store may be needed to meet shoppers' desires.

People in a big church want the nurture, love, and support of a small group where they're known—much like the fellowship common in a small church. They want the senior pastor to know and care about them. They want to feel they are part of and are important to an extended family.

The senior pastor needs to help the congregation create many opportunities for people to get involved in projects they care about. Then they can build nurture groups around the things that unite them.

It's important when fostering these groups to expand on the strengths. People want to be part of something that's working. They want to feel like winners. Provide lots of opportunities for people to see successful, concrete ministry being done.

Learn the traditions and use them for the vision

Each church has its own traditions, and they're all different from those in every other church. In a big church especially, these traditions may be rooted in stone, and a pastor must learn quickly which traditions are not to be tinkered with. The most vital traditions can range from upholding the liturgical pageantry, which is the church's hallmark in the community, to the pastor's expected attendance at certain annual events sponsored by particular groups.

It can be a good idea to have what one pastor calls a "godfather"—someone who will fill you in on the history of different events. A conversation with a previous pastor, a longtime staff member, or the church council may help you learn congregational history.

Once the vital traditions of a church are identified, examine what roles they may have played in past visions. Can these roles be successfully transplanted into the church's current vision? It's great if everything a church does makes sense, from the way the candles are lit to the type of anthems the choir sings, to where they spend the bulk of their money. If things don't make sense, you may need your creativity to work the various parts into a coherent whole.

Getting the staff on board

You will probably inherit a staff. They need to understand early how their responsibilities may change or grow under your leadership.

Waneta was the new senior pastor of First Church. She was the church's first female senior pastor. She had heard that some of the staff at First Church were not happy with her appointment. They weren't sure they wanted to be led by a woman.

She held a staff meeting the first week. During the meeting, Waneta told the staff she expected them to be loyal to her, to the church, and to the vision of the church's ministry as it developed. She coordinated their perceptions of their jobs and of her responsibilities. She told them she wouldn't rescue them, that she'd let them do their work in their way. She would not interfere unless they asked for help.

The staff was not used to such direct language, but they appreciated knowing where she stood. They understood that they had a strong leader in Waneta, and that they needed to be willing to follow her.

It's always a good idea to be clear with your staff. If they have different priorities from yours, the church will suffer for it. If you are all going in the same direction, the church will prosper under the team guidance.

A good staff makes a senior pastor's life much easier. They bear responsibilities that are usually those of the pastor alone in smaller congregations. This frees up the senior pastor to spend more time on sermon preparation (often seen as the main duty of a senior pastor) and on research and development of specific areas of ministry. Knowing you can count on your staff to get things done is the great luxury of the big church.

Representing the church in the community

Though all pastors are asked to officiate at civic events from time to time, pastors of big churches find they are often called on. They may be expected to be on the platform at local college graduations, be visible at community charity events, and belong to at least one secular service organization. Don't let the community call on you so often it affects your attendance at church events. You may want to set a policy of how often you will attend or officiate at civic functions.

Whenever you do attend civic events, people will be watching to see what kind of pastor the big church has. They will likely judge the entire congregation by the public persona you project. Getting self-conscious yet?

Living with the reality

There is a quote often heard from big-time pastors: "When you hit the big time, you'll find out who your friends really are."

It's sad but true that some pastors have a jealous nature. When they see a colleague getting a pulpit or position they thought they were in line for, they may not be able to remain friends with that pastor.

In some cases, these friendships are lost, not through jealousy, but through the intimidating nature of the new position. A big-time pastor's friends may think, *He's so busy now. I won't call him. He won't have any time for me.* These friends need to call precisely because the pastor is so busy. They need to remind their friend to save time for them, to relax in a group where it's okay to be yourself.

Another common quote from big-time preachers says, "In a big church, there are a lot more problems."

They're not making this up, or trying to assuage the jealousy of less-than-big-time colleagues. Large churches often have more dissatisfied people than small churches do. It's not that the percentages are higher, it's just that there are more people within each percentage grouping. Many of these dissatisfied people are also very vocal.

The big-time pastor has to get used to dealing with these folks. There are many more compliments, but also many more complaints in a big-time church. It's not a place for the fainthearted.

In addition, while the big time pastorate does have rewards, it may also have the most demanding schedule of any church around. What's important is for the senior pastor to build a true picture of the church, see that it's headed in the right direction, and develop the proper skills to help the church reach its goals.

The best advice

One piece of advice comes from the twenty-year pastor of a *very* big time church. At various times throughout his ministry, he has made a point of asking himself, "Am I still having fun?"

That's the main thing. Have fun. Enjoy your job, big time or not.

17

Even Elvis Had a Hound Dog

We had dinner once with a pastor and his wife who had just retired after more than forty years of ministry. They had moved several times and his career had advanced with each move. They were a lively, enjoyable, highly regarded couple. Theirs seemed to be a success story.

The dinner went well; we all enjoyed each other's company. Afterward, while we were waiting for dessert, the wife leaned forward to give us some advice. "We made some lovely friends at different churches we served," she said. "They were people we hated to leave. But when we left, we left. We cut off all relationships and each church was a fresh start. We'd been advised that this was the way it should be. We didn't want to interfere with the following pastor's work."

She glanced at her husband, who was looking down silently at his empty plate. "Now we have few friends," she said. "All those years, all those wonderful friendships we ended, people we loved and who loved us—we simply abandoned them." She touched my hand. "Don't let that happen to you. Keep your friends. You won't be their pastor any longer, but you can still be their friend."

What a tragedy that this couple was entering retirement with such a sense of emptiness and loss. Their advice is valuable. Don't be a pastor to your friends after you leave. Don't perform their funerals, baptisms, or weddings, unless as a mere—and fully welcome— assistant to their current pastor. Don't listen to or encourage their conversations about the state of the church since you left. Don't give advice about the church or its programs. But do keep the friendship alive. Do send cards and stay in touch by letter. Do keep your friends.

Making friends in a new place

It's easy to make friends when we're children. We just go up to someone and say, "Want to play?" When we become adults, things get more complicated. Especially for pastors. People just don't see us as potential playmates. It's up to us to initiate most new friendships.

How do you invite people to play? Let's say you're in a new town and new church. It's Friday night and you're ready to party. But you don't have any friends here yet. How do you quickly get into the social life of a new place?

Having people over for dinner is one way. Of course, most of us don't feel much like entertaining the first few months after we move in, but it's often the easiest way to establish friendships.

Church friends

When Sylvia and David had been at their new church two weeks, they chose three couples in the church whom they felt would mesh well with their family and with each other. The three couples were all invited over for dinner on the same night, each being informed that the others were coming.

The guests arrived on time and conversations began to flow. The dinner was going well, and all seemed to be enjoying themselves in a restrained sort of way. Toward the end of the meal, one guest asked, "So why have we all been called together?"

David was surprised. "For dinner," he said.

"But what's the agenda?" the man persisted, looking a bit concerned.

David looked at Sylvia. She smiled and shook her head. "No agenda. You just seemed like a fun bunch. We thought we'd like to know you better."

The group relaxed after this and enjoyed each other's company so much they still make a point of getting together for dinner every so often. It was a good mix and the beginning of good friendships.

The most discouraging thing about being a pastor and inviting people over for dinner is that you often have to welcome people two or three times before they understand you're not just being nice. Knowing it's your job to be nice, they may not take your invitations at face value. So be persistent. If you sense a kinship with people, pursue it. If friendship is a real possibility, they'll finally come around.

Some people will tell you that it's impossible to have close friends in a church, that they will confuse you with your role as pastor and will at times presume on the friendship. Don't we all presume upon friends from time to time? If we know a chemist, don't we ask her if we have a question concerning her field? If we get together with a lawyer, don't law and taxes occasionally work their way into the conversation? If we frequently have coffee with an English teacher, won't we ask him about a point of grammar?

So what if our friends occasionally address us in our pastoral role instead of our personal friendship role? Everyone does that. We shouldn't be offended by it.

There *are* limits to friendships with church people. A key limit, for instance, is that generally we dare not share personal struggles or frustrations related to congregational life. To do so may feed our reactions back into the congregation and intensify our troubles (and the congregation's) through a kind of deadly feedback loop. But if in church friendships we can avoid congregational issues or interfering with another clergyperson's ministry, the rewards of such relationships can be significant.

People also say that making friends within a church invites jealousy and comments about favoritism. Although this may happen, it's a losing battle to try to be noncontroversial. Of course, you won't talk to your friends exclusively at church gatherings, ignoring other members. And you certainly don't want to mention private get-togethers in public. But this is all just common sense. If you hit it off with people in church, don't be afraid to invite them over. You may be at the beginning of the most rewarding relationships you'll ever have.

Nonchurch friends

What about making friends outside of the church? They're great if you can get them. But they are hard to come by.

Sometimes you will get to know people through common interests, such as community clubs or sports events. These friendships need special nurturing, but they can be renewing and relaxing. They may also go deeper than many church friendships, which may not move to an intimate level.

If you make a friend who is totally outside of any church, consider yourself lucky. This person will teach you a lot about the secular world, some of which you won't want to hear. You will likely be valuable in your friend's life too, bringing a different perspective to common ideas. In many ways, it's like getting to know someone from a different culture. You will be challenged and occasionally find yourself doing the challenging. If the relationship survives, it will become something truly special.

Preacher friends

Of course, it's easiest to make friends among those with whom we have much in common. Some of our best friends are other pastors and their spouses. They understand our life and we understand theirs. We can gripe to each other, knowing we will be heard correctly, and nonjudgmentally. We can celebrate small triumphs with them and reveal our failures, as well as share theirs. Make it a priority to get to know several local pastors. If any seem to strike the right chord, invite them to dinner. You just might click.

When to go slow

It is natural to want to fit in and meet new people. Occasionally, however, clergy find they have to put the brakes on a relationship that seems to be propelled by something other than just a desire to get to know the pastor.

Marlene was a single pastor in her first rural charge. Having grown up in a city, she was a bit uneasy about the different life and culture she found herself in.

The first Sunday she was there, the church threw a "pound party" for her. Everyone brought a pound of something to the parsonage—a pound of hamburger, a pound can of beans, a pound of tomatoes. Marlene was happy at this welcoming. And she was pleased to meet Jane, a married woman a few years older than Marlene, who was friendly at the party and invited her over for lunch the next day.

The relationship got off to a good start. Jane offered to help Marlene get acclimated to the area and rural lifestyle. Feeling welcome, Marlene began spending a lot of time with Jane's family. They filled her in on church history, the various personalities, their version of what was wrong with the congregation. Marlene realized they often gave advice she hadn't asked for, but she tried to brush it off. After all, they meant well.

One evening warning bells finally started going off for Marlene. Jane and her husband suddenly revealed personal problems in the former pastor's life. Marlene tried to change the subject. She really didn't want to know the intimate details they were revealing and said so.

Jane nodded as Marlene protested. "That's what I like about you, Marlene, you are so nonjudgmental."

Marlene smiled with relief that she had finally gotten them off the subject of the former pastor.

Jane went on. "We'd just like you to know that as we were Pastor Hunt's special confidantes, we'd like to offer you the same thing. We know the ministry is a hard life. Sometimes you just have to let everything out. So, honey, we're here. Anything you want to share, just go right ahead."

"That's okay," Marlene said, suddenly aware that Jane and her husband seemed very eager to have her "share." "No problems so far."

"Oh, Marlene, you can tell us. Aren't there a few people in church who just get to you? That you'd just like to strangle? Come on, it's okay." Jane leaned forward, smiling.

Marlene felt herself leaning backward. "Oh, look at the time. I promised two people I'd drop by tonight. If I don't leave right now, I won't have time to make it." She got up. "Sorry I have to leave so soon. Dinner was great."

She finished her good-byes and hurried out of the house. She was painfully aware that if Jane and her husband hadn't first revealed the former pastor's confidences, she could easily have been persuaded to do a little wholesale complaining. She felt like a sucker. She realized that Jane hadn't really wanted *her* as a friend, but that Jane had wanted the *pastor* as a friend.

Jane liked being in the know. Being the pastor's buddy was a good way to get a sort of vicarious power over the rest of the congregation. Marlene was careful around Jane and her husband from then on, and took everything they said with a handful of salt.

How do you know when to be wary? It's hard, but there are a couple of indications that friendships may not be developing as they should. Be careful around those who—

1. **Are too anxious to know you.** These aren't the people you hit it off with and whom you want to be around anyway. These are the people who actively pursue you and with whom you don't feel all that comfortable. Try to discover their agenda.

2. **Are too impressed with you.** If they love your sermons, think you are a saint, and are impressed with your standing in the denomination, be careful. They probably aren't relating to you, just to your professional trappings. And unfortunately, people who run hot also tend to run cold. If someone falls in love with you immediately, they can change their mind just as quickly. All it takes is one mistake. When you reveal that you are not a saint, they may see this as a betrayal.

Have no regrets

A surprising truth is that we have different friends for different activities. With some we celebrate. With some we take risks. With some we reminisce. With some we discuss politics. With some we do sporting activities. And with some we share our deepest selves. The more friends we have, the fuller our lives. Get friends. Love them. And keep them. You'll never be sorry.

18

It's Time to Get Out of Dodge

How do you know when it's time to leave a church? That's a tough one. Some pastors feel a need to move on every four or five years. They've settled into an itinerant lifestyle and are uncomfortable if their feet are too long on the ground in any one place. Others can stay at the same church for twenty years and feel better about it each succeeding year.

So how do you know when you need to move on?

Here are a few clues that may help you decide.

1. You have no energy. We're talking here about having no energy for church work as well as general depression. You're just going through the motions. You're physically and mentally exhausted.

2. The challenge and fun are gone. You realize that minor things are taking up most of your time. You don't enjoy the things you used to.

3. Your skills have been used up. You haven't started a new program in a long time. You have settled into doing maintenance rather than pointing toward new possibilities.

4. It's harder to deal with apathetic people. Too often you find yourself agreeing with them that "nothing ever changes around here."

5. Your own spiritual life feels parched. You're not getting anything out of your sermons and wonder if anyone else is. Bible study has become a chore rather than a time of inspiration.

6. Your denominational supervisor, spouse, or friends tell you it's time to go. They see that no matter what you do, things at the church are not going to change significantly. They also see that you are too close to the situation to look at it objectively.

If any of these clues hit home, give yourself time to contemplate a move. If you're sure moving is not the answer, you may want to get into counseling. Except for number six, all of the above clues are also signs of depression.

Why is depression so closely related to the need to move? It could be because moving is a time of change and we always resist change. We often go into a period of mild grief at any significant change, even if the change is a welcome one.

After all, it's not easy, taking everything you own, packing it in boxes, loading it on a truck, and sending it off to some place where you'll have to build a new life. Even if you're delighted to get out of your present situation, it still isn't easy. However, there are ways to make departure more bearable, if not actually enjoyable.

Decide it's a good idea

First, make up your mind that it's a good thing to be moving, even if you have no choice in the matter and secretly believe it's a mistake. After all, life is a process of going forward, not remaining stagnant. So—think about it, pray about it, discuss it with your therapist, your mother, your spouse. Look for reasons why the move is a good thing at this stage of your life. If you decide the move feels right, your stress will decrease.

Make the decision privately

Don't feed any rumors prior to a definite decision.

Gary and Denise, a pastoral couple, were considering leaving the rural church they had served for six years. They had seen the congregation nearly double in size and become a vital, loving community. However, a sameness and sense of restlessness had overtaken the couple. They were struggling with whether to move.

One Sunday they hosted a pastor friend as their guest speaker for the evening worship. In the church office before the service, they asked him to pray with them about their struggle. Afterward they felt some comfort but did not feel they had yet come to a decision. An hour later that choice was taken out of their hands.

Their friend gave a stirring sermon. The congregation had risen for the last hymn when the preacher raised his hand to stop the pianist. "Please pray for your pastors," he said. Gary and Denise stood in shocked disbelief as he repeated to the congregation everything they had told him in private just before the service. He ended by asking the congregation to pray that their pastors would make the right choice.

The church members were devastated at the realization that their pastors wanted to leave. Feeling betrayed, they reacted in hurt and anger. Many lashed out at Gary and Denise immediately following the service. Others sent letters the following week or came by the office to voice their anger and disappointment.

The effective ministry of this couple was over at that church. It was another six months before the actual move took place, but the time was a hard one for both parties. The congregation felt abandoned; the pastors felt pain and guilt.

This type of experience is possible if a move is mentioned as a possibility rather than as a decision already made. Some pain will surface in any move, but it's easier for a congregation to deal with a leave-taking that is already settled than one that's just a possibility.

Inform as few people as possible ahead of time

If a decision has been made to move and you have some dear friends in the congregation, you may want to tell them about the move ahead of time. Do this only a day or two before the public announcement. Your friends deserve a private conversation with you, but it's unfair to ask them to keep such a secret for a long time. Do choose carefully whom you tell. Understand that we are talking about dear friends here, not just casual dinner partners.

Plan carefully how you will tell your children

Children never want to move. That's a given. They don't want to leave their school, their friends, their activities. And who can blame them?

As soon as you know you're moving, tell your children—that is, if they're old enough to keep it secret. When you do tell them, be prepared to let them show their frustration. They may react with tears, anger, or both. That's okay. They may even show the classic grief response of denial: "I won't move. I'm staying here." Help them progress through this grief. Let them get over the first shock, then talk with them about how you can help make it more acceptable for them.

It's easier for children if they're not expected to make a clean break. Arrange ways for them to see old friends, maybe complete their season on the softball league.

Moving during the summer can be especially hard on children. After all, they'll make most of their friends at school. That first summer they have a lot of time on their hands and no one to spend it with.

Use the transition period to let your children know how special they are to you, how much they are appreciated as part of the family. Try to provide all the reassurance they need. Don't fail to take a vacation. The new church may want you there all summer, but your children desperately need the family time to feel nurtured and cared for.

Let an authority figure make the formal announcement

The decision to move has been made, and it's time

to inform the church at large. Now what? You may want to have someone else, such as the pastor-congregation relations committee chair, make the announcement of your leave-taking. This can take place on a Sunday morning at the end of the worship service. Even if you're happy about going, this will be a moment of intense stress. Let someone else do the dirty work.

Your specific congregation and denominational polity can guide how far in advance you make the announcement. One to two months is appropriate in many settings, but a considerably longer period may be helpful in other situations.

Have the person making the announcement tell the congregation the date you'll be moving and where you'll be going. You may not want to get into the why's of the move. At this point the date and new location may be all the information the people need and can absorb. Something should also be said—now or as soon as appropriate depending on your congregational setting—about how soon a meeting or interview with the incoming pastor may take place.

The speaker needs to be positive. This is not a tragedy (though well-meaning church members will try to tell you it is). It is merely a time of change and growth, for both you and the congregation.

Mental leave-taking

Once the decision to leave has been made, let yourself see what you've accomplished. Be glad about it. Pat yourself on the back. Then mentally let go of the programs, the triumphs, the office, the new computer you talked them into, the parsonage. This will soon become a part of your past. These things won't matter in your future life except as memories.

Be prepared to deal with the grief— both yours and theirs

Don't be surprised when, after the announcement, people in the congregation seem newly discontented with you. That's part of the grief process. No one likes change, and one way to deal with it is to become angry. You may become the focus of that anger. Try to see it as part of the leave-taking. It really isn't personal, though it often feels as if it is.

Now may also be a good time to clear the air over old disagreements. After all, you're leaving, and you can try to leave on good terms. It can be a source of great healing to ask forgiveness for past mistakes or animosities, or to offer forgiveness by attitude and action to those whom you may feel have wronged you.

Don't be surprised at your own grief. Even if you're delighted with the move and the prospect of a new church, it's common to find yourself in the midst of unexplainable sadness, or to wake up in the night suddenly afraid you've made the wrong decision. These are both signs of grief—the grief of change and of having to adapt to a new situation.

Give yourself the freedom to talk about the move with people. Share the grief. Celebrate the good memories. Be honest—but not unkind. Don't say you're glad to go, even if you are.

A baffling but common result of an announced move is that a flock of people may suddenly ask you out to dinner. We're not talking about close friends here, but mere acquaintances. It seems they had always meant to get around to having you over, and now the time is short.

Don't feel compelled to accept all these invitations. Go to the ones you really care about and have the energy for. These last-minute meals are a way of saying good-bye, of bringing closure. See if you need closure with all these people. If not, and you're too busy to accept, they'll probably be satisfied with a hearty thank-you and a few minutes of conversation.

Don't underestimate the time it will take to pack. A three-bedroom house cannot be packed in an organized manner in under two weeks. It cannot be packed well in under a month. Two months is better. Don't rush yourself at the last minute. It's not worth it.

During the last month

Now your life is composed of hundreds of details you must handle. Streamline as many as you can by making a list early in the month and getting to work on it right away.

At church it's time to pack your books. Leave out only those you know you'll need for your last few sermons. Consider using several days to write some of those last sermons ahead of time, so you have more time for the actual moving work.

Go through your files, separating your personal material from church material. Many pastors move into a new church to find that the former pastor has taken everything, from the financial statements down to the memberships lists. They have to work months to get back even the basic information that should have been left behind in the first place.

It's time-consuming but also rewarding to go through the files carefully. Many things will come to light that will be useful in future churches—special programs, innovative ways of running stewardship drives, and so forth. Copy everything you think you may use, then replace the originals in the church file.

Be good to your successor

Some pastors feel that they shouldn't leave any clues behind for the next pastor. They want him or her to find out everything firsthand—who's in charge of the annual turkey dinner, who's a good typist in a pinch, and other helpful details. Be kind. Write these hints down. The new pastor may or may not find this material useful, but it really isn't fair to keep this information to yourself.

Joe, a pastor in his early thirties, was replacing a retiring pastor. A few weeks before Joe arrived, he wrote a letter to the retiree, asking him to make a list of the church leaders and workers. Joe also hoped for the retiring pastor's opinion of the congregation's financial situation and its general attitudes concerning such issues as stewardship and evangelism. The retiree refused. He sent the younger man a letter telling him he'd have to make those discoveries for himself.

One can see the logic in the retiree's letter. Different pastoral personalities do result in changes in the church leadership. It's unwise to prejudice a new pastor for or against church members. However, it's also unwise to invest several years of your life in a congregation and not leave behind some aids to the next person's fruitful ministry.

Joe did soon discover who the church leaders were and who the good volunteers were. But it was nearly a year before he learned the congregation had an endowment of over two hundred thousand dollars whose existence the finance committee had kept secret from the congregation. It was unkind and unwise of the retiree to keep this information from the new pastor.

Passing on the care

One piece of useful information is a list of names and dates of church member deaths which occurred during the previous year. Families need and appreciate a call on the anniversary of a loved one's death.

One pastor found this out by accident, when in the space of a month he happened to call on three widows on or near the anniversary date of their husbands' deaths. They each mentioned the significance of the date and were eager to speak to the minister, to share memories and renew their faith. He found these to be among the most meaningful calls of his ministry.

Let your successor know when certain people may especially need to be ministered to. Include a list of shut-ins and others who may need fairly immediate care by the new pastor.

Final days

Don't over-schedule yourself at work this last week. Let the church work go. Your main responsibility at this point is to get yourself moved out. Delegate everything you can. After all, you won't even be here next week. They can get along without you and it won't hurt them to discover that fact a week early. This may seem unnecessary advice, but some congregations want to hold onto their pastors until the moving truck pulls out of the driveway.

In their separation anxiety, some people may come up with sudden emotional problems that need your counseling expertise. Others may decide to unload their years of bitterness on you. You're leaving. You're safe. They won't have to see you again, nor deal with the results of their actions if they tell you off.

These kinds of experiences may never happen to you, but they do to many pastors. It's good to be aware that this is part of the separation anxiety. Participate in contacts caused by separation anxiety only if you see potential for healing.

Turn away from situations that may only breed hurt. If you feel this may be a problem, be unavailable. Don't make appointments. Refer those with emotional problems to the local mental health professionals. If you find yourself in a bitterness-unloading situation, be tactful, but don't take time to listen. Leave. At this point, you already have all the stress you can handle.

This week is also when your close friends will want to have you over for dinner once more. It's good to be with them, but you'll feel panicked over your move and all the last-minute details you have to take care of. If your friends volunteer to help you pack, accept gracefully. You can use the help, and it will assist them in accepting your move and feeling useful. It's also a good time to plan your next get-together at your new place.

Time for the adventure

You've made a tough decision. You've worked through the grief. You've done closure. You're physically out of the house and office. The moving truck is on the road.

Now you're ready to continue your ministry in a new place, with new friends and challenges. Let the grief of change go for a moment. Savor the excitement of this new life in front of you. You're moving on.

19

A Pastor's Bill of Rights and Responsibilities

As ministers, we can get caught in an in-between place, so involved in our duties and so aware of other people's expectations that we feel we have no real rights. This is especially true in our early churches. Wanting to do a good job, we may try to satisfy everyone. Since this is impossible, we often end up unhappy with our jobs and ourselves, realizing too late that we didn't know where to draw the line in defining our own boundaries.

We hope this list of rights helps you draw your own lines. Be aware, though, that this list has to be modified to fit you and your situation. If one of these rights does not fit your situation, discard it. Add other rights to the list if helpful.

A PASTOR'S BILL OF RIGHTS

****

A pastor has the right to—
- enjoy her job
- enjoy his family
- a private life
- a social life outside the congregation
- have close personal friends
- enjoy holidays
- cry
- laugh
- take vacations
- take days off
- set her own hours
- preach without undue interference or censorship from others as to content or topic
- recreation
- a passionate love life with his spouse
- a decent place to live
- furnish her house in whatever manner and style she sees fit
- choose his own wardrobe without consulting others as to what is appropriate
- raise her children without interference from her congregation
- his own hairstyle and facial hair
- privacy in her own house or in the parsonage
- think about his career and future and to plan for them
- save her money

- spend his money however he decides is appropriate
- keep her finances private
- buy any car he likes and can afford
- get angry
- be sad
- get counseling for emotional and mental problems
- get sick
- argue
- celebrate private family times
- make family needs a priority
- private spiritual devotional time
- outside interests and hobbies
- move
- refuse to answer personal questions
- ignore petty complaints
- change his mind
- express her own opinions
- refuse to perform weddings if he feels he has sufficient grounds
- insist on particular rules in any wedding she performs
- refuse to counsel certain individuals and to refer them to others
- set his own priorities in the performance of his ministerial duties
- pursue higher education and continuing education
- be active in community affairs
- take risks
- say no.

****

Along with any list of rights also comes a list of responsibilities. We often think these responsibilities go without saying, but maybe they need to be stated. Here's the list. You may want to add to it. We don't recommend deleting anything—but again, your situation is unique.

A PASTOR'S LIST OF RESPONSIBILITIES

****

A pastor is responsible for—

- seeing that church services begin and end on time
- her own spiritual health
- working at least forty to fifty hours per week for the church (if full-time) and more hours when the situation demands
- carefully preparing a sermon for weekly worship
- providing counseling for church members or directing them to someone who can
- seeing that an attitude of worship is maintained during services
- maintaining a friendly, nonjudgmental attitude toward each member of her congregation
- visiting the sick in his congregation, or making arrangements for others to do it if the burden is too heavy for one person
- seeing that the administrative and programming goals of the church are theologically sound and ministry based

- praying regularly for her congregation, both individually and collectively
- providing leadership and guidance to his congregation
- teaching membership classes and encouraging new members
- performing baptisms
- officiating at funerals
- serving communion (in most denominations)
- maintaining the highest ethical and moral standards in her own life
- donating as much as he can to the causes of the church
- keeping her personal finances in order
- planning and providing for his retirement income
- keeping a church-provided parsonage clean and avoiding damage to it
- taking days off and for setting and taking vacations
- maintaining a high level of personal hygiene
- seeing to her family's needs and giving them frequent quality time
- taking care of his physical and mental health
- preserving the happiness of her marriage
- listening to his congregation
- keeping confidences
- her own mistakes
- his own career
- her own happiness

****

The Authors

Deborah Bushfield was born in Indianapolis, Indiana, in 1954. She was educated at the University of Evansville (Ind.) and Indiana University (Bloomington) where she earned an M.F.A. in Creative Writing. She has taught writing courses at the University of Indianapolis, Indiana University, and Indiana University/Purdue University (Columbus, Ind.). Her work has appeared in *The Louisville Review* and *The Business Network*.

As the wife of a United Methodist pastor, Deborah has lived all over southern Indiana and has been part of ten congregations, ranging in size from fifteen to 900 members.

She and her husband, James, presently live in Bloomington. Deborah teaches at Indiana University's Creative Learning Center, convenes the Bloomington Writer's Group, and works on a wide variety of projects as a freelance writer.

James Bushfield was born in Indianapolis in 1952. He

was educated at Indiana University as well as at United Theological Seminary (Dayton, Ohio), where he earned an M.Div. (1972) and a D. Min. (1992). He received his doctorate, under the direction of Thomas Boomershine, in biblical storytelling and preaching.

James has taught preaching at the 1992 Hoosier Gathering, the 1993 Global Gathering, the Cincinnati School of Religion, and a number of district workshops. He gave the keynote address and was primary workshop leader at the 1993 Indiana Pastors' Conference at Christian Theological Seminary.

In recent years James has been the Conference Relations Registrar with the South Indiana Conference of the United Methodist Church's Board of Ordained Ministry. He became chair of the board in 1993. He has been a key member of a conference committee designing orientation procedures for new pastors.

James has served churches in southern Indiana since 1973 and was ordained an elder in 1980. He has served nine congregations and is currently pastor of the Fairview United Methodist Church in Bloomington.